TEACHING WITH CLARITY

Other ASCD Books from Tony Frontier

Effective Supervision: Supporting the Art and Science of Teaching

Robert J. Marzano, Tony Frontier, and David Livingston

Five Levers to Improve Learning: How to Prioritize for Powerful Results in Your School

Tony Frontier and James Rickabaugh

Making Teachers Better, Not Bitter: Balancing Evaluation, Supervision, and Reflection for Professional Growth

Tony Frontier and Paul Mielke

TEACHING WITH CLARITY

How to Prioritize and Do Less So Students Understand More

TONY FRONTIER

Alexandria, Virginia USA

1703 N. Beauregard St. • Alexandria, VA 22311-1714 USA
Phone: 800-933-2723 or 703-578-9600 • Fax: 703-575-5400
Website: www.ascd.org • Email: member@ascd.org
Author guidelines: www.ascd.org/write

Ranjit Sidhu, *CEO & Executive Director;* Penny Reinart, *Chief Impact Officer;* Genny Ostertag, *Senior Director, Acquisitions and Editing;* Julie Houtz, *Director, Book Editing;* Jamie Greene, *Editor;* Thomas Lytle, *Creative Director;* Donald Ely, *Art Director;* Keith Demmons, *Senior Production Designer;* Kelly Marshall, *Production Manager;* Shajuan Martin, *E-Publishing Specialist;* Christopher Logan, *Senior Production Specialist*

All web links in this book are correct as of the publication date below but may have become inactive or otherwise modified since that time. If you notice a deactivated or changed link, please email books@ascd.org with the words "Link Update" in the subject line. In your message, please specify the web link, the book title, and the page number on which the link appears.

PAPERBACK ISBN: 978-1-4166-3007-4   ASCD product #121015   n6/21
PDF E-BOOK ISBN: 978-1-4166-3009-8; see Books in Print for other formats.
Quantity discounts are available: email programteam@ascd.org or call 800-933-2723, ext. 5773, or 703-575-5773. For desk copies, go to www.ascd.org/deskcopy.

Library of Congress Cataloging-in-Publication Data

Names: Frontier, Tony, author.
Title: Teaching with clarity : how to prioritize and do less so students
   understand more / Tony Frontier.
Description: Alexandria, VA : ASCD, [2021] | Includes bibliographical
   references and index.
Identifiers: LCCN 2021007381 (print) | LCCN 2021007382 (ebook) | ISBN
   9781416630074 (paperback) | ISBN 9781416630098 (pdf)
Subjects: LCSH: Teaching. | Teachers--In-service training. | Learning,
   Psychology of. | School improvement programs. | Academic achievement.
Classification: LCC LB1025 .F87 2021 (print) | LCC LB1025 (ebook) | DDC
   371.102--dc23
LC record available at https://lccn.loc.gov/2021007381
LC ebook record available at https://lccn.loc.gov/2021007382

30 29 28 27 26 25 24 23 22 21   2 3 4 5 6 7 8 9 10 11 12

*For my parents. They showed me how to wonder,
encouraged me to try, listened to me while I struggled,
and then humbly asked me how I'd learned.*

TEACHING WITH CLARITY

How to Prioritize and Do Less So Students Understand More

Preface

When I started writing this book in early 2019, there were three questions I knew would be central to the text:

- What does it mean to understand?
- What is most important to understand?
- How do we prioritize our strategic effort to help students understand what is most important?

I've asked these questions hundreds of times to thousands of educators over the years. I'm always impressed with the depth and thoughtfulness with which individual teachers and administrators answer the first two questions. However, even among teachers working in the same schools or departments, they tend to answer the first two questions in very different ways. This makes responses to the third question very complicated. It is difficult to help students prioritize when we haven't established our own shared priorities.

In the absence of shared priorities, we are making a choice to do more work and attain fewer results. Unfortunately, rather than acknowledge this conundrum as a failure to prioritize, it is usually diagnosed as a failure to put forth enough effort. Teachers and students assume—or are told—that the reason the outcomes they seek haven't been attained is because they just *aren't working hard enough*.

Teachers rise to the challenge by searching for more materials, resources, and activities to make class time more productive. They do more, cover more, assign more, give students more options, test more, and grade more. "Good students" comply . . . yet there is little evidence that *covering more* or *teaching more* results in more learning. For students who struggle to keep up, we double down and ask them to do *even more*. Ultimately, this response only increases their frustration and our exhaustion.

At some point, it's as though "busyness"—rather than learning—became the purpose of schooling. Frustration is accepted as a proxy for high expectations, and exhaustion is worn as a badge of honor.

Then, in March 2020, the busyness of teaching in classrooms around the world came to a complete stop.

During the COVID-19 pandemic, many of the tools and resources used for teaching were taken away, but the expectations for learning remained. It was difficult. It was stressful. Helping students thrive in this new context required less busyness and more clarity. Take away the busyness of the activities and coverage that dominate most school days, and the three questions that would guide this book were all that remained.

It is said that crises don't create weaknesses—they reveal them. On its surface, schools' responses to the global pandemic revolved around the twin crises of instructional delivery and technology access. At a deeper level, it revealed a crisis about how schools prioritize and clarify the shared expectations that guide students' strategic efforts for learning. If schools acknowledge technology-related challenges but fail to clarify and align their priorities for student learning, then—once we reach a post-pandemic world—we'll have merely added *online learning* as another tool to deliver and access more busyness, frustration, and exhaustion.

The central questions of this book haven't changed since its inception. I argue that incremental changes over the last 30 years mean clarity about what it means to understand—and what is important to understand—is more important than ever. The dramatic challenges we all faced during the pandemic revealed an urgent need to discard a lot of the clutter that fills our school days and distracts us and our students from effective teaching and deep learning.

This book is about choosing clarity.

1

Understanding Clutter

This book is going to be challenging for you. If it were easy, I would simply ask you to do more, but as educators, I know we're already good at that. Indeed, in my years as teacher, administrator, researcher, and consultant, I've never been in a school or district where everyone wasn't already working hard. Everyone is busy; everyone is pursuing the next initiative.

In our pursuit of better meeting the needs of every child, entire systems are busy implementing new math or reading programs, or they're establishing equity and social-emotional learning programs, or they're setting up formative assessment systems or response to intervention programs, aligning curricula to state standards, or implementing new report cards. Or they're doing everything at the same time.

In short, the underlying message is clear: *We're not quite there yet because we haven't added the right program.*

Teachers today are more adept at accessing and searching through information and resources than at any other time in human history. Somewhere out there on the internet is the next lesson idea, rubric, video clip, article, activity, performance assessment, assessment bank, incentive system, or bulletin board idea that might be better than the one you're currently using (or you might find the magic solution that gets kids to put down their phones). The temptation to find these mythical solutions is real, but the underlying message is clear: *We're not quite there yet because we haven't added the right resource or project.*

So why will this book be challenging for you? Because I'm going to ask you to do *less*.

If doing more in our schools and classrooms were the answer to better meeting the needs of every child, then we'd have met every goal and closed every gap by now. We don't need more activities, resources, projects, assessments, or meetings. We need more *clarity*.

Clarity emerges when we prioritize our efforts to do less with greater focus. With this focus, we give our students time to prioritize their efforts and develop deeper understanding. The enemy of focus is clutter, which is anything that inhibits our ability to help students prioritize their strategic efforts to learn. Clutter is what happens when we do more with less focus. With clutter, there is never enough time or energy to find success; there is always more to cover and more to do. The first step on the path to clarity is eliminating the clutter we put in front of kids during the 16,380 instructional periods they experience in a typical K–12 education system.

Clarity begins to emerge when systems have the discipline to collectively answer three questions:

- What does it mean to understand?
- What is most important to understand?
- How do we prioritize our strategic effort to help students understand what is most important?

If we can't provide clear answers to these questions, then no one in the system can prioritize—or align—their effort to their strategy. And when you try to accomplish something (whether it's in school, at work, or with a hobby), a disconnect between your effort and strategy will almost always result in frustration or failure. What you mistakenly internalize as an ability problem (i.e., I tried hard, but I'm just not good at that), an effort problem (i.e., I guess I'm just not trying hard enough), or a time problem (i.e., I'd like to do that, but I don't have time) *is actually a failure to prioritize strategic effort.*

Prioritizing and aligning strategy to effort is a challenge for all schools and teachers. However, this challenge requires educators to identify and overcome a set of misguided assumptions about improvement that are out-dated and rooted in the Industrial Age.

The Industrial-Age Problem (and Irony) of Organizational Clutter

During the Industrial Age, organizations and laborers worked to turn raw materials into a product of value. A passive set of raw materials would roll down an assembly line and get pieced together along the way. If everyone did his or her job right, a finished product emerged. If the product was of poor quality, the solution was to reorganize—the assembly line was restructured or the organizational chart was modified.

Schools today are still organized according to this somewhat archaic industrial model. Twelve years of formal education, class periods, and the accumulation of credits are an invention of the Industrial Age. According to this model, if we want a better product, then we need to structure things differently: we need to slow down the assembly line, ring the bells at different times, or ask workers to put in overtime. This Industrial-Age metaphor for restructuring schools to improve learning is clearly misguided, yet it persists. In *Five Levers to Improve Learning,* Jim Rickabaugh and I argue,

> Too often the effort put forth, the political chips spent, and the resources allocated to make these structural changes result in few, if any, meaningful differences in educational practices or student learning. . . . Changes such as moving to a block schedule, adding more computers, or developing a new report card fit neatly into strategic plans, and their implementation processes have clearly defined starting and ending dates. However, we argue that these types of changes often produce the least amount of leverage in terms of improving student learning. (Frontier & Rickabaugh, 2014, p. 10)

These changes rarely prioritize efforts to be more strategic at the point of contact between the student and teacher. Therefore, we conclude,

> Efforts focused on large-scale reform haven't been successful because those efforts have failed to change schools. They haven't been successful because, too often, the transactional, structural approaches that can change schools have little or nothing to do with the less visible but far more powerful strategies

required to change students' learning experiences in those schools. (Frontier & Rickabaugh, 2014, p. 164)

Ironically, rather than improve students' learning experiences, we've merely added to the system or made it more complex. Unfortunately, administrators often fail to realize they've merely contributed to *organizational clutter*. They've changed the system, yes, but they haven't built new capacity for students to strategically focus their efforts to learn.

The Information-Age Problem (and Irony) of Curricular Clutter

A curriculum is a sequence of learning experiences designed to help students achieve a goal. In the Industrial Age, schools were expected to produce individuals who had the knowledge and skills to contribute to the economy and be a part of a literate, informed citizenry. Teachers directed students along a path to give them the opportunity to gather and learn the information that would make them educated.

In the early 1900s, schools and universities were of value because they were *the* organizations that could provide students with access to that information. If students paid attention and learned, the return on their investment would be to contribute to the economy and democracy. However, as newspapers, magazines, radio, and television became more and more easily accessible fixtures of American society, information became accessible everywhere and to everyone.

Nobel Prize winner Herbert Simon (1971) explained the gravity of this change:

> In an information-rich world, the wealth of information means a dearth of something else: a scarcity of whatever it is that information consumes. What information consumes is rather obvious: it consumes the attention of its recipients. Hence, a wealth of information creates a poverty of attention. (p. 40)

In the 50 years since Simon made that observation, the internet and cell phones have steadily increased the wealth of information available to each of us at an astronomical rate. Indeed, Simon couldn't have imagined the vast wealth of information, or the corresponding poverty of attention, that exists today. Not only is there more information available, it's more easily accessible, and because there are no barriers to entry for posting something online, large amounts of the information is of lower quality. However, this only addresses a symptom of an even deeper challenge.

As Tim Wu (2016) explains in *The Attention Merchants,* in an era of unlimited information, the most powerful companies in the world exist to get people to pay attention to *their* information. The cumulative result, he argues, is that we are all in a state of constant distraction. In 1971, Herbert Simon saw a "wealth of information." Today, there is wealth in information. More than ever before, *information is a product, distraction is a marketing strategy, and attention is the economy's most profitable commodity.*

As educators, I don't think we've fully acknowledged how this commoditization of information and attention has changed the relationship between students and schools. When information is a profitable product that is accessible everywhere, *the battle for kids' attention is everywhere.* Schools are no longer the exclusive spaces where students go to access important information and acquire skills so they can one day be hired by Industrial Age companies, such as Shell Oil or Ford.

Today, access to information is occasionally about schools and learning, but more often it is about eyeballs, page views, and clicks. As we prepare students to be successful in the Information Age economy, we compete with companies like Google, Apple, and Facebook to get students to pay attention to *our* information. Every day, these companies efficiently facilitate the millions of pages of new content and become more effective in their use of strategies to garner attention. Clutter and distraction aren't bugs in the system; they are its central features.

Ironically, in our quest to get students to pay attention, we immerse ourselves in the same sea of clutter that is also the source of our students' constant distraction. Google searches for "rubrics" and "lesson plans" yield nearly 100,000,000 results. It's no wonder we're endlessly searching the internet for the next interesting article, video clip, lesson idea, activity, or easy-to-use rubric. But as we click on those links, do those new resources create clarity for learning, or do they create more clutter?

Choosing Clarity: Shared Purpose and Process

What are the choices we make each day to build a system that makes sense from the students' perspective? When this question becomes a habit of mind among teachers and administrators, kids notice. It helps teachers acknowledge that their individual efforts are less important than how they focus their collective energy to help kids prioritize their efforts to learn. In his book *Essentialism,* business consultant Greg McKeown (2014) states, "Our highest priority is to protect our ability to prioritize" (p. 101). That's a powerful statement for both personal and organizational growth, but how can it be applied to schools to create clarity amidst the clutter?

I'd like you to envision a system in which principals, teachers, and students all have the same answers to the three questions about alignment of understanding, strategy, and effort that I previously posed. Now imagine those principals, teachers, and students have one—and only one—priority to support that system. Consider the following six statements.

Clarity of Shared Purpose

- We have a shared understanding of what it means to understand.
- We have a shared understanding of what is most important to understand.
- We prioritize our use of time and strategies to support students' strategic efforts to develop important skills and understandings.

Clarity of Process

- Administrators' highest priority is to protect and develop their teachers' ability to prioritize.
- Teachers' highest priority is to protect and develop their students' ability to prioritize.
- Students' highest priority is to prioritize their strategic effort to learn what's most important.

When this level of clarity is pursued as a system, both teachers and students are the beneficiaries. Less clutter translates to greater focus and more time and effort to pursue what is most important. Clarity is a strategic choice, and you must be willing to do less by investing focused effort on what is most important.

As educators, we like to think we've already prioritized what is most important in our schools and classrooms. We haven't. This book will help you understand why. This book is about focusing our collective efforts on the learning that matters most, creating systems that help students understand what those things are, and empowering students with the tools to focus their strategic efforts to improve. Not surprisingly, we'll connect educational research to best practices. Six elements of clarity will be used to guide our efforts. We'll also apply some powerful metaphors for prioritization drawn from fields ranging from medicine to mountain climbing, ideas for decluttering drawn from tips for tidying one's home, and elements of design used to make your phone so easy to use.

The first step on the path to clarity is acknowledging that we have a clutter problem. To better understand this problem and how to address it, we need to consider what clutter looks like through a student's eyes.

Understanding Clutter: Questions for Discussion and Reflection

- As a school, how have we clarified for students what it means to understand?
- As a school, how have we clarified for students what is most important to understand?
- As a school, do our initiatives typically result in doing more or in focusing our efforts to do less more effectively? Explain.
- How well do we prioritize our use of time and strategies to guide students toward the most important understandings? What evidence points to our successes? Challenges?
- How might students benefit if they were clearer about where, and how, to invest in their strategic efforts to learn?

The Clarity Paradox

Why do students see clutter where we see clarity? If we are going to better understand the clutter problem, then we need to get a better understanding of how students perceive the problem.

As the leaders of one of the world's foremost design firms, David Kelley and his colleagues at IDEO have developed a multiphase, collaborative process to develop products and solve problems called *design thinking* (Kelley & Kelley, 2013). One of the key elements of the design thinking process is empathy—the ability to see a system, product, or problem through the lens of others. To be empathetic is to understand and value how another perceives and experiences the world. By contrast, a nonempathetic approach assumes others perceive and experience the world exactly as you do. Between empathy and the absence of empathy is sympathy, which is an acknowledgment of another's feelings (often, of sadness or frustration when they cannot control outcomes).

An example of the results of empathetic design can be seen in IDEO's design of a child's toothbrush. An adult taking a nonempathetic approach might assume a child merely requires a smaller version of an adult's toothbrush and simply has to muddle through. An adult taking a sympathetic approach might look at the child with pity and assume he or she cannot accomplish the task him or herself. To prevent frustration, the adult grabs a toothbrush and brushes the child's teeth. By contrast, an empathetic approach considers how a child actually holds a toothbrush. Whereas adults hold a toothbrush with their fingers, children typically hold them in their clenched fists. Counterintuitively, a design with a much thicker handle is more suitable to how children intuitively grasp a tool designed to clean their teeth.

Likewise, when planning learning experiences for students, an empathetic design approach can be used to better understand how students perceive our classrooms and schools.

Through the Eyes of Our Students

Let's consider the problem of clutter in schools from nonempathetic, sympathetic, and empathetic design perspectives. A nonempathetic approach to tackling the clutter problem might be for educators to ask, "Where am *I* experiencing clutter in my school day?" They would then solely look for ways to streamline their workload. A sympathetic approach might prompt this response: "Students must be really stressed with all the work they're expected to do. I should give them less work, and the system should give them access to more socioemotional support." An empathetic approach, by contrast, would begin to address the clutter problem by understanding how school looks through the eyes of a student. Here, educators ask, "As students move from class to class, day after day, how do they know where to invest effort to succeed?"

An empathetic approach to instructional design is not new. For example, in Rick Stiggins's seminal work on student-centered classroom assessment, he implores teachers to see "assessment through the eyes of students" (2007, p. 22). Even though *we* may see assessment as a process to guide decisions about student achievement or to inform our next efforts to support their learning, students may see it as a judgment of their ability to attain standards they are powerless to achieve. To transcend this, Stiggins (2001) advocates for assessment that helps students "see and understand the scaffolding they will be climbing as they approach those standards" (p. 327).

John Hattie also advocates for an empathetic approach. In his synthesis of educational research in *Visible Learning for Teachers* (2012), Hattie says the entire field of educational research can be captured in two phrases. Learning occurs most effectively "when teachers see learning through the eyes of the student and when students see themselves as their own teachers" (p. 238).

In other words, students learn best when we acknowledge that they don't already know what we know and don't wake up thinking about our lesson plans. Once we've learned something, it's easy to forget there was a time when we didn't understand it. The best teachers transcend this conundrum. They acknowledge that what may be clear to us—what high-quality work looks like, nuances among easily confused concepts, the definitions of certain terms—may not be clear at all to students.

Most of the sage advice from Stiggins, Hattie, and other researchers who have built on their important work tends to focus on what teachers need to do in their classrooms to see learning through the eyes of their students. This helps teachers understand the challenge of instructional clarity, but it does not help teachers adequately address the problem of clutter. With that in mind, I want us to take Stiggins's and Hattie's advice a step further to understand how our complacence with individual clarity can inadvertently result in clutter for students. Rather than just thinking about your classroom, ask yourself this question: "How does an entire K–12 experience look through the eyes of a single student?" Answering this question requires us to be empathetic not only to how students experience your classroom but also to how they experience the system as a whole.

An Exercise in Empathy: The System Through the Learner's Eyes

Consider the following thought exercise to empathize with how students may perceive their K–12 schooling experience. Suppose you are hired to teach in a new district. As part of a three-day orientation session, your principal tells you about her deep commitment to supporting each teacher's professional growth and the amazing administrative team with which she works. There are several orientation and team-building sessions with your principal, instructional coaches, administrators, and other new teachers. The culture is professional and collegial, and you get the sense that they all care about you as an employee, a teacher, and a person.

On the afternoon of the third day, your principal walks you through the process she will use for evaluation. She shares the rubrics, dates, and deadlines; she describes the constructivist philosophy behind the approach; and she does a great job explaining specific look-fors, the rubrics she'll use, and how final ratings will be determined. Then she introduces the assistant principal—who will also be evaluating you. However, the assistant principal shares a very different process and a more didactic philosophy, and he explains the different, specific things he'll be looking for. He then introduces the personnel director who shares yet another process, approach, and set of rubrics. Ultimately, this happens four more times. Two administrators say they don't use rubrics because they evaluate "for content, not skills." One administrator says he'll be looking for "a lot of integrating technology because it is the essence of 21st century teaching," whereas another thinks technology "is detrimental to learning." All of them use different formats, templates, and processes that are then converted to a common evaluation scale.

As you start to wonder how you are going to keep up with all these different systems, you are told that all seven administrators will be visiting your classroom every day. You start looking around the room, wondering if the other new teachers are hearing the same words you are. They look equally perplexed. Then, to your surprise, you are told that next semester, there will be seven more administrators with different approaches, rubrics, processes, and philosophies. You are assured that you don't need to worry; they will let you know their expectations before the semester begins. Finally, you are shown a slide of the *more than 90 administrators* who will be visiting your classroom over the next 12 years. Beneath the slide, a caption reads "Supporting teachers to be reflective, lifelong learners in a 21st century school!" You can feel your pulse quicken.

At this point, the superintendent comes into the room. He looks at the slide and gives his own testimonial. "I just want to say I can't think of a more talented or harder working group of administrators in the state, and they bring a wealth of experience and knowledge to our system and to you." Everyone in the room seems competent, skilled, and professional, yet you wonder, shouldn't the system have a coherent sense of what high-quality teaching looks like? Shouldn't the system adopt a few powerful sets of descriptors that can be used to clarify—rather than create clutter?

As the school year progresses, you become frustrated as you try to keep up with the competing evaluation systems, rubrics, and processes. Your principal wants your "learning goal" written on the whiteboard each day. Another evaluator wants your "learning intention" on the bulletin board each day. A third wants your "learning target" posted online each day, a fourth wants your "intended target" on a daily assignment sheet, and a fifth prefers an inquiry-based approach where students establish a "guiding question" each day. The expectations for lessons diverge even further—each evaluator wants a different structure, uses different vocabulary, and applies a different approach. You have a hard time keeping focused amidst the clutter and are left feeling frustrated.

Eventually, you muster up the courage to talk to your principal. She greets you at her door and genuinely asks you how your weekend was. When you describe your weekend, you get the sense that she is really listening. After the pleasantries, you share a bit of your frustration concerning the range of expectations from your evaluators. She sympathizes and tells you about some of her own struggles from her first years of teaching. She then reexplains *her* system. For clarification, you ask if a "learning goal" and a "learning intention" are the same thing. She's visibly surprised you asked. She says she thought you did a great job describing your learning goals in your first post-conference meeting and seems unaware the other evaluators don't also call it a learning goal.

She encourages you to spend more time preparing your lessons to alleviate the anxiety. She asks if you'd like to process some of what you are feeling with one of the instructional coaches. You thank her and leave to schedule a meeting with the instructional coach. At an administrative meeting the next day, your principal tells the admin team that you seem overwhelmed and wants feedback so she can better help you succeed. They all tell her you are working hard and showing a lot of effort. One administrator mentions a new program he's heard about to address the stress experienced by new teachers. The team thinks the program sounds like it is worth pursuing. A few weeks later, you receive an invitation to join a support group for new teachers that meets for an hour every Tuesday afternoon.

If you were this teacher, how would you feel? When I've done this exercise in workshops, common responses I hear are *overwhelmed, confused, frustrated, exhausted,* and—without a bit of irony—*cared-for* and *supported.*

The Clarity Paradox

The previous thought exercise is designed to support empathetic understanding of what I call the *clarity paradox.* It is counterintuitive to expect everyone within a system to be clear about their expectations and show genuine expressions of care for those they serve while those who use the system feel overwhelmed, confused, and neglected. Nevertheless, this happens in systems all the time. Like any paradox, the clarity paradox consists of two true, yet contradictory, claims:

> *Each individual within the system perceives clarity.*
> *Those who use the system experience clutter.*

Understanding the clarity paradox reveals the futility of a variety of ways systems usually react when there is a disconnect between effort and results. Too often, those who lead or work within an organization assume the confusion must be related to a deficiency in the people who are served. Out of concern, they respond by adding more clutter. *We are working really hard, and we really care! The problem must be that the people we serve need another program, more technical support, more emotional support, and more rewards and consequences!* None of these responses addresses the root cause of the problem: a lack of clarity within the system.

The clarity paradox rests on a series of false assumptions about the role of professionals within large systems:

1. **The false assumption that professionals within an organization have the right to assess and apply assessment criteria in any way they choose.** Imagine finding out your parent or grandparent with a heart condition has been seeing a physician with "her own

way" of determining and measuring blood pressure, and she has been using a completely different method and scale than internationally accepted protocols. The essence of a profession is that the individuals within that field assess for important indicators of quality in very similar ways. Professionals operationalize their judgment and expertise to help those whom they serve achieve shared, rigorous standards for quality. They don't simply create their own standards.

2. **The false assumption that complex skills and understandings cannot be defined or assessed because they are too subjective.** If the expertise within a system cannot establish a shared language and articulation of what high-quality work looks like, how can novices within the system invent a disciplined understanding of what they don't know they are supposed to pursue?

3. **The false assumption that it takes too much time to develop a shared understanding of quality and articulate clear success criteria because everyone is too busy and there is not enough time.** This is a bit like saying, "I'm too tired to get this flat tire fixed tonight because I have to wake up early and drive to a critically important meeting tomorrow morning." A system that is too busy to strategize in order to clarify its most important results is a system that is designed to frustrate, rather than accelerate, the learning of those who use the system.

As you no doubt noticed in the teacher evaluation example, the clarity paradox is obvious. When we are held to account with ambiguous language and ever-shifting expectations, we become frustrated. However, when we are one of many individuals who are empowered to establish and apply our own labels and expectations for high-quality work, we don't notice how we are contributing to the clutter. To reveal the clarity paradox in schools, we must step back far enough to see not only our classrooms but also the entire system through students' eyes.

Revealing the Clarity Paradox in K–12 Schools and Classrooms

What does the clarity paradox look like for students in schools? As one component of my work and research, I help schools and districts review, develop, and align curriculum. Typically, when districts begin this process, I meet with the principal or director of learning for an initial conversation. Regardless of the size of the school or district, and whether it is urban or rural, the stories they share tend to be similar. The staff works incredibly hard and administration has stretched the available resources as far as possible, yet everyone in the school community believes students can do even better. The schools are engaged in a flurry of important initiatives: RTI, PBIS, Equity, PLCs, instructional coaching, socioemotional learning, standards-based grading, project-based learning, culturally responsive instruction, implementation of new standards . . . to name just a few.

Then they tell me about the new curricular programs they are implementing, or they guide me through an internal curriculum management page and show me what they have established (or not established) as related to developing curriculum. This is where the schools and district differ. They tend to fall into one of three categories:

- Some have adopted books and programs but have no formally established curriculum.
- Some have mapped out standards and adopted resources—and may even have a standards-based reporting tool—but alignment among the various elements is superficial and transactional. For example, there may be spreadsheets that list where all the curricular standards are "covered" and a formal inventory of what instructional materials are used, but no elements are in place to implement the potential of these plans into classrooms.
- Some have delved deeply into curricular design, using an intentional approach in which units are established and articulated in terms of

standards, key outcomes, specific projects, and resources. They are "standards-based" and may have had a standards-based report card for many years.

For each of these systems, I always ask the same question: "Can you send me copies of the rubrics teachers use in their classes?" After asking this question, I typically hear the same response:

"Like, all the rubrics we use across all grades?"

"Yes," I reply. "Writing rubrics, math and science practices, historical inquiry . . . anything teachers use to assess work that can't simply be marked right or wrong."

There is a pause, and then I hear, "Let me see what I can do."

Several weeks later, I typically receive an email with dozens of attachments, a link to a 74 gigabyte shared folder, or a manila envelope the size of an old-school telephone book. I review the contents, and regardless of where that school or system is in the curriculum development process, I reliably see the following:

- Dozens (sometimes hundreds) of rubrics from some subject areas— primarily language arts courses—fewer rubrics (usually for specific projects) in social studies and science, and almost no rubrics from mathematics courses.
- Rubrics from a wide variety of sources. Some are copied from textbooks or teacher guides, some are made by teachers, some are from national discipline-based organizations, and many are printed directly from online sources.

Looking across these rubrics from a single school or distrct, patterns emerge that reveal the clutter problem and the clarity paradox. For example, categories of focus and the language of success criteria appear random and arbitrary, and descriptors of quality and levels of expectation vary from teacher to teacher, rubric to rubric, and course to course:

- **Category names are arbitrary:** For example, science rubrics may label categories as *claim, evidence,* and *reasoning* on one set of rubrics and *hypothesis, data,* and *rationale* on another. Across a single school's writing rubrics, categories related to identifying the main idea of an essay may be labeled as *thesis, purpose statement, opening statement, topic statement, establishes topic, attention grabber, lead, intro,* or *introduction.*

- **Academic language is used arbitrarily and sometimes even contradicts itself within the same rubric:** Words such as *describe, explain, tell* and *summarize, analyze, synthesize* are used as though they are interchangeable.

- **Categories describe tasks rather than attributes of quality:** For example, categories such as *PowerPoint, poster, heading, elements of a lab report, number of sentences,* and *neatness* are often followed with descriptors about arbitrary elements of a task that have little to do with quality as related to standards.

- **Different levels of success criteria are used across a seemingly random, broad range of terms:** Within a single school, levels of quality may be described as *does not meet, beginning, below basic, basic, developing, approaching, emerging, progressing, some understanding, meets expectations, meets standard, on-level, advanced, sophisticated, beyond expectations, beyond grade level, very good, exceeds expectations, exemplary, expert, above grade level,* or *way above grade level.*

- **Criteria for discerning levels of success are based on arbitrary values or terms**: For example, *"lists 3 examples"* for *proficient* and *"lists 4 examples"* for *advanced* or *"shows some thought"* for *meets expectations* and *"shows a lot of thought"* for *exceeds expectations.*

- **Rubric layouts vary in their structure:** Criteria may be listed in a checklist; a list of bullet points; or tables with three-, four-, or five-point scales.

- **Rubric organization is not consistent:** Lower-level (basic) criteria may start in the left column and flow to the right with higher levels of quality (complex), as in *Level 1, 2, 3, 4.* However, sometimes higher-quality descriptors start on the left and flow toward the lower levels on the right, as in *Level 4, 3, 2, 1.*

- **Rubric formatting is all over the place:** Sometimes criteria are listed in columns (*Level 1, 2, 3, 4*) and categories are in rows (*claim, evidence, reasoning*), and sometimes criteria are in rows and categories are in columns.
- **Titles and labels don't describe the assessment tool . . . or agree with one another:** The document header may be labeled as *rubric, success criteria, assessment rubric, grading rubric,* or *grading scale.* The columns (or rows) could be labeled as *points, scale, criteria, grade, categories, standards, indicators, elements, components,* or *power standards.*

The Effect of the Clarity Paradox on Teachers and Learners

As I observe the variability in the rubrics described in the previous section, I ask myself the three alignment questions we discussed in the first chapter:

1. What does it mean to understand?
2. What is most important to understand?
3. How do we prioritize our strategic effort to help students understand what is most important?

The first two questions are addressed in the individual rubrics but in dramatically different ways across the system. All teachers put forth a lot of effort, all teachers care, and all teachers can justify their expectations for quality. However, through the eyes of students, the answers to these important questions appear as arbitrary, moving targets from task to task, class to class, and teacher to teacher. This then leads us to the third question, which is where I get a knot in my stomach.

As students move between and among assignments, classes, subjects, and teachers, how do they recognize and understand what high-quality writing, scientific reasoning, or historical thinking looks like? If we aren't clear about what is most important and if we aren't clear about what high-quality work looks like, then students find themselves reacting to what they see as a clutter of conflicting expectations, directions, descriptions, and scales.

The ramifications of the clarity paradox on students' ability to demonstrate evidence of understanding cannot be overstated. *What students may perceive to be an ability problem, or what teachers may diagnose as an effort problem, is actually a clarity problem.*

In the teacher evaluation thought exercise we walked through earlier in this chapter, the teacher had enough expertise to see that the system was cluttered. The teacher was aware of—and could be metacognitive about— the disconnected elements of the evaluation system. However, 12-year-olds don't have the capacity to see their confusion and frustration as a systems issue. Therefore, they self-diagnose an ability issue. *"I'm trying hard, but I don't get this. My teacher keeps showing me stuff, and I keep trying harder, but I still don't get it. I guess I'm not very good at subject X."* In other words, students can't be strategic about improving at a complex academic skill— such as writing, problem solving, mathematical reasoning, analyzing data, or making arguments from evidence—if they believe the most important ways of thinking within a discipline and the pathway to understanding that discipline are both arbitrary.

If we are truly going to see the problem of clutter as students do, we have to be empathetic enough to see *the entire system* through their eyes. Regardless of our individual capacity to teach effectively, if we aren't clear *as a system* about what high-quality work looks like and what matters most in each discipline, then it is tantamount to educational malpractice to ask students to figure it out for themselves.

Balancing Structure and Autonomy: How Different Systems Use Constraints to Create Clarity

To eliminate clutter and transcend the clarity paradox, we must find a different mental model for balancing individual autonomy and shared expectations for quality. Effective systems strive for a balance between organizational structure and individual autonomy. This is done by deciding where to place constraints and on the expectations for what individuals will, and will not, do to prioritize their efforts to ensure clarity.

A system with no constraints is chaos. In fact, it's not really a system at all; it's a random collection of individuals creating clutter and ignoring the clarity paradox. Conversely, if a system embraces too many constraints without ensuring the time, capacity, resources, and skills to ensure everyone can meet them, then the system merely acts as an enforcer to micromanage each member's compliance.

Maximal Structure, Minimal Autonomy: Clarity Through Many Constraints

An orchestra playing classical music is an example of maximal structure and minimal autonomy. In classical music, the musicians agree to play the exact notes as written on the page. If there are 800 notes and 40 musicians playing parts for 12 instruments, there are hundreds of thousands of instance of overlap. When we factor in the rigid structure of time, pitch, and volume, there are millions of nonnegotiable constraints. When the musicians embrace every constraint, clarity emerges and beautiful music happens. If they break the agreement, then the structure turns into clutter because each musician didn't do *exactly* what was expected. For example, if the flutes make a recurring error in measure 42, the entire orchestra has to go back and fix it. In this high-structure, minimal-autonomy system, the *nonnegotiable constraint is that for clarity to emerge, every note has to be played in the right way, at the right time, and for the right length for each piece of music.*

Systems with maximal structure and minimal autonomy can be successful if the system has the time, resources, expertise, and supports necessary to ensure every constraint is embraced and accomplished with precision and accuracy. A professional orchestra can rehearse a piece and play it to perfection. But if each musician doesn't play each note exactly as written, the errors become glaring.

Schools can often feel like systems of maximal structure and minimal autonomy but without the time or coordination necessary to turn those constraints into clarity. In an effort to improve student learning, administrators often add more constraints to cope with the clutter that ensues—more expectations, more accountability, more assessments, more files and forms—and afford less autonomy. As much as teachers lament this, they often do the same thing to their students; they add more expectations, more content, more tasks, and less autonomy. Caught in the middle, students cope by trying to just play the right notes each day—or at least avoid playing the wrong ones in a way that others notice. Eventually, students come to believe the system is about doing as much as you can, making as few errors as possible, and then moving on to the next thing. When everyone is playing a lot of notes but there are too many of them to provide the support and focus necessary to play the music as written, it results in a discordant cacophony. What else can be done?

Minimal Structure, Maximal Autonomy: Clarity Through Prioritized Constraints

When I am not consulting, researching, or teaching, I am a musician. I play piano professionally. I've performed with dozens of musicians whom I'd never met until the moment we started making music in front of a live audience. How is this possible? We accepted and adhered to only a few constraints. We were playing jazz.

Jazz musician and leadership guru Frank Barrett (2012) describes jazz as a system of "minimal structure and maximal autonomy" (p. 67):

> Jazz bands are a 'chaordic system,' a combination of chaos and order. The critical design element for jazz bands and for leaders is the nonnegotiable constraints that need to be in place so that chaos can lead to creativity rather than something undesirable. (p. 68)

The premise of jazz music as one of minimal structure and maximal autonomy dispenses with all but a few of the millions of constraints required in the classical music example. Rather than agreeing on every note to play, jazz musicians agree to prioritize their efforts of *what to play* and *what not to play* by using a shared language and deep understanding of just four nonnegotiable constraints: key, tempo, mode, and chord progression. Jazz musicians agree *how to play* by using two nonnegotiable constraints: you take turns leading (soloing) or comping (backing up the soloist). With this in place, the shared language and meaning of the prioritized constraints can generate millions of opportunities for creative freedom, yet the system still works as intended. There is no need to control every note; the six constraints are built around what is most important to understand and allow each musician to prioritize their efforts in a manner that can be fluidly transferred from one performance to the next.

Like jazz, schools thrive with a deep commitment to a few, powerful nonnegotiable constraints. *Why?* A complete absence of constraints makes things impossibly chaotic; by contrast, too many constraints creates impossibly high expectations for perfection. Like jazz, prioritized, nonnegotiable constraints to guide decisions about teaching and learning can minimize the need for excessive structure, maximize autonomy, and allow for creative freedom. But where should schools focus their efforts to establish those prioritized constraints?

Creating Clarity: Align Assessment Evidence to Priorities for Learning

The most efficient way to change learning experiences is to align strategic efforts for teaching to the most important outcomes for learning. Biggs & Tang (2011) expanded on earlier research (Tyler, 2001) to share a clear synthesis of where to focus our effort and where to prioritize around a few constraints that are most likely to improve learning in schools. They argue that if students aren't learning at the rate or depth we desire, it's important you

- Don't blame the students.
- Don't blame the teacher.
- Don't blame the teaching tool.
- *Do* blame the lack of alignment.
- *Do* blame the lack of aligned assessment. (Biggs & Tang, 2011, p. 48)

Most curricular issues, student learning issues, instructional materials issues, teacher effectiveness issues, and instructional time issues are actually symptoms of a lack of clarity and a lack of alignment of expectations to what is most important to learn. Confronting the clutter and addressing the clarity paradox doesn't require us to do more. Rather, it reveals an urgent need to prioritize our efforts around a manageable number of nonnegotiable constraints. If we aren't clear about what it means to understand and what is most important to understand, then it is impossible for students and teachers to align their strategic efforts to improve.

How can constraints be used to ensure autonomy and improve results? In the next chapter, we look at an example of an assessment system that committed to five constraints. In the process, they eliminated clutter, addressed the clarity paradox, and empowered professionals to improve results for hundreds of millions of children.

The Clarity Paradox: Questions for Discussion and Reflection

1. Stand in the shoes of a student in your school. What is an important process related to teaching and learning where you think teachers see clarity but students experience as clutter?

2. Stand in the shoes of a student in your school. What is a skill in which students believe they have an academic ability problem—but that is, in fact, a clarity problem?

3. How do we currently use prioritized constraints to focus students' attention toward an understanding of the most powerful and transferrable understandings in each discipline?

4. How might students and teachers benefit if we were able to more effectively align expectations across grade levels and disciplines? What if we could more effectively align our instruction to what is most important to learn?

3

From Clutter to Clarity

In Search of Clarity: The Surprising History of the First Assessment You Ever Took

In 1880, life expectancy in the United States was 40 years. Fortunately, because of hundreds of breakthroughs in medicine, science, and public health during the 20th century, that number nearly doubled by 1950 to an average life expectancy of 70 years (Statista, 2021).

Tragically, despite the tremendous medical breakthroughs that nearly doubled life expectancy, the infant mortality rate did not change over that time. Between 1880 and 1950, one in every 30 infants died at birth (Gawande, 2007). Some physicians accepted this rate as biological destiny—*children are fragile, deliveries can be complex, you're expecting too much.*

Among the cadre of better-trained physicians who graduated from medical school in the first half of the 20th century was a woman who transcended the limitations of gender stereotypes and sexism to become a medical doctor. She established a successful practice in the emerging field of anesthesia and found working in birthing rooms to be the most rewarding—and challenging—part of her practice. When she saw how physicians and birthing teams responded to infants born under duress, she was shocked at the variability in professional practice.

As she observed this variability, she realized that infant mortality wasn't an effort problem or a technology problem; it was a systems problem. Simply put, there was no systemic way for birthing teams to respond to an infant born under duress. As she probed further, she realized the root cause of the systems problem was an assessment problem. There wasn't a focused, shared understanding of what it even meant to be born healthy. Consequently, the expectations, processes, and protocols to respond to the unique needs of each birth were unfocused and ambiguous. In short, she saw clutter and no constraints.

Over a period of three years, the anesthesiologist developed an assessment to help birthing teams understand the most important attributes and indicators of what it meant to be born healthy or under duress. The assessment required no special equipment, minimal training, and observations related to just five components: respiration, heart rate, muscle tone, skin color, and reflex. It was administered one minute after birth and again five minutes after birth. Each attribute was scored on a simple but reliable 0–2 scale. It produced meaningful results that birthing teams could use to respond to infants' needs in real time.

She published her research on this simple assessment in 1953. In 1962, two physicians slightly changed the semantics of the five components to *appearance, pulse, grimace, activity,* and *reflex.* They argued that a simple acronym—APGAR—would make the five components easier to teach—and pay tribute to its creator, Dr. Virginia Apgar.

Aligning Strategic Effort Through a Shared Understanding of the Most Important Evidence

If you were born after 1953, the APGAR assessment was likely the first assessment you ever took—or, more accurately, it was the first rubric used to assess you. It revolutionized the field of obstetrics. For the first time, physicians had a shared understanding of the most important evidence related to an infant's health and what it meant to be born healthy. Because everyone was looking for the same five meaningful indicators along a reliable scale of success criteria, important evidence wasn't missed or ignored. With valid, reliable data in hand, physicians could do research and collaborate on the causes and effects of complications during each delivery. The health of an infant was now an objective, rather than subjective, measure. Through the application of APGAR scores, purposeful methods of response based on babies' needs in each important area were established. Clutter and reactivity were replaced by clarity and intentionality. The five priority items and a common scale—all nonnegotiable constraints—provided the focus required to improve outcomes and afford autonomy.

From 1880 to 1950, the infant mortality rate had remained around 1 in 30. Fifty years after the publication of Apgar's assessment, that rate for a full-term pregnancy improved to be *1 in 500* (Gawande, 2007, p. 187). Apgar saw how clutter and the clarity paradox prevented systemic improvements to healthcare and meeting the needs of newborn babies. What had been accepted as a problem with *the child* was revealed to be a problem of *the system* and its inability to prioritize and focus on what mattered most.

For the first time, teams of physicians and nurses could say

- We have a shared understanding of what it means to be born healthy.
- We have a shared understanding of the most important indicators of an infant's health.
- We prioritize our use of time and strategies to look for, and support, the most important evidence related to each infant's health.

At no point did Virginia Apgar—a humanitarian who went on to lead the March of Dimes—say, "*Healthy* is subjective and can't really be assessed" or "Because each child is unique, you can't measure what is most important." To the contrary, she found that the ambiguity and lack of clarity in the system's understanding of what "healthy" looked like had created a field primarily engaged in talking about methods of resuscitation rather than one committed to identifying success criteria that could prevent complications in the first place. (For more information on the history of the APGAR assessment, see Apgar, 1953; Finster & Wood, 2005; Gawande, 2007).

Assessment can be objective without being cold and uncaring. What matters is how the information brings clarity to people working within the system and helps them better align and focus their efforts to be of service to others. When assessment is done well, it is the antidote for clutter and the catalyst for clarity.

Six Assessment Components That Create Clarity for Teaching

The story of the APGAR assessment is one of systems-level clarity (see Figure 3.1). The team of medical professionals who welcomed you into the world was *focused* on a manageable set of prioritized indicators. They were *intentional* about gathering the assessment evidence that mattered most. They made *reliable* inferences about the meaning of important evidence. The results were used as *meaningful* feedback in real time so they could exercise their professional expertise to be more *purposeful* and *responsive* to your needs.

Given the anecdote about the APGAR assessment, consider the following scenarios about four different hospitals. Read carefully; after you've read them, I'll ask an important question that will draw your attention back to students and schools.

- **Scenario 1:** *We're all professionals who care about children, but we can't control what happens before they come to the hospital.* You are an obstetrician who arrives to work in a new hospital. You ask the hospital administrator about the use of APGAR data. The administrator replies, "All of our physicians use different assessments; we're all professionals here and we all care about kids, but they all look for different characteristics. Some kids just don't make it. It's heartbreaking, but we can't control what happens before they come here."

- **Scenario 2:** *We already collect a ton of data that are reported to the state and presented annually to the board.* You are an obstetrician who has been recruited to work in a hospital. You ask the head physician what protocols are in place for APGAR data. The head physician responds, "The state collects our mortality data in February, we get it back in May, and then our administrators report the results to the board in July, so we don't need the APGAR." He continues, "Besides, the physicians and nurses never really looked at the results anyway."

Figure 3.1

Characteristics of Assessment Systems That Choose Clarity

Elements of Clarity	How the APGAR Assessment Demonstrates the Criterion
Focused: Prioritization of success criteria as aligned to the most important standards	Of hundreds of possible variables, it is focused on five of the most important observable categories.
Intentional: Gathers the most important evidence as aligned to the most important standards	It directs everyone's attention to the most important evidence to ensure accurate, useful information about an infant's needs as related to the focused success criteria.
Reliable: Consistent inferences about the relationship between evidence and success criteria	Everyone can make similar inferences about an infant's needs by consistently linking the most important evidence to the most important success criteria.
Meaningful: Shared understanding of how evidence relates to success criteria is used to respond to feedback in meaningful ways	The inferences are used to provide meaningful feedback—in real time—about an infant's needs, to inform an effective response.
Purposeful: Success criteria and aligned assessment process clarify shared purpose	Everyone in the system uses the assessment information for a common purpose: to communicate priorities and take action to support each infant's health.
Responsive: Assessment evidence gives focused, meaningful information to guide strategy and effort	Everyone in the system uses the assessment information to align strategies to prioritized efforts to be responsive to infant's needs.

- **Scenario 3:** *We're aware of the standards, but parents only really care about height and weight.* You are an obstetrician who has been assigned to a new birthing team. Over lunch, you ask a new colleague about the use of APGAR data. She replies that the staff did an APGAR training a while ago, but they were "looking for those types of things already so we didn't use it much." You press her a bit more and she lowers her voice and says, "I didn't really give low APGAR scores because it would make the parents in this community angry. Parents here only care about height and weight."
- **Scenario 4:** *Because the child's well-being is our first priority, we have a shared understanding of how the most important evidence aligns to*

the most important success criteria in real time, and we constantly focus on those prioritized indicators to guide our efforts to improve. You are an obstetrician interviewing for a position at a hospital, and you are seated at a large table with six members of the hospital staff. Before the interview begins, you are given a single sheet of paper that outlines the hospital's nuanced version of the APGAR assessment; brief definitions that establish a shared language of key terms; and a short summary of the *who, what, when,* and *how* pertinent to the data's use. You'd noticed several poster-sized versions of the document in each birthing room. The administrator running the interview says, "Here's our team. They'd like to share their roles with you and ask you some questions; then you'll have a chance to ask them questions." She turns the interview over to a nurse seated across from you. The nurse says, "We use the APGAR to focus our collective efforts to be more responsive to the infants we serve. . . ."

Given these scenarios, where would you send a loved one who is expecting? If these were schools with analogous systems of assessment to support student learning, where would you want that child to attend? By most accounts, the first three scenarios are appalling. Professionalism is seen as the right to assess as one chooses, failures are dismissed as the fault of others, data collection is seen solely as an accountability task to serve administrative needs, shared criteria for quality are merely assumed, and appeasing parents' feelings is deemed more important than an infant's health. There is maximal autonomy but no shared constraints. Individuals may be competent, but absent a clear focus on what matters most, everyone is working hard to achieve random results. These hospitals have fully embraced the clarity paradox.

The final scenario is markedly different. This hospital's focus on prioritized criteria for quality provides clarity for how staff can work together to serve children. It is a systemwide expression of care: *we have high standards, we have clear criteria, we focus on the most important components, we know just how to respond, and we are honest about how we will use assessment evidence to help us get even better.* This hospital has accepted an empowering, shared set of prioritized constraints—it has chosen clarity.

As a school, how have you prioritized the most important evidence? What is your shared understanding of how that evidence aligns to the most important success criteria in the disciplines you teach? What is your shared language of quality? Do you have an APGAR equivalent in each discipline that prioritizes your efforts to teach—in real time—and your students' efforts to learn?

"We" Statements That Align to the Six Assessment Components

When teachers have a shared understanding of what assessment evidence is most important and what high-quality instruction and learning looks like, they are empowered to prioritize their strategic efforts to ensure students can prioritize their efforts to learn. To develop students' ability to prioritize their efforts, teachers can create clarity by embracing six constraints:

- **Focused, Shared Success Criteria Aligned to Prioritized Standards:** We have a shared understanding of what high-quality work looks like as related to prioritized standards. We use a published, shared proficiency scale to communicate success criteria for a manageable number of standards across courses and grade levels to support each teacher's, and student's, ability to monitor progress toward mastery.

- **Intentional Design of Standards-Aligned Assessment Prompts and Performance Tasks:** We have a shared understanding of how to design assessment tasks that provide accurate evidence of students' understandings of priority standards. We use a shared language of rigor based on our common proficiency scale to ensure all assessment tasks produce valid evidence of the most important knowledge, skills, and reasoning as related to priority standards.

- **Reliable Inferences About Student Learning Based on Valid Evidence and Success Criteria:** We make accurate inferences about what assessment evidence says about student learning, based on our prioritized standards and shared success criteria. We acknowledge the complexity and importance of making valid inferences about student understanding based on observable evidence and the success criteria.

- **Meaningful Feedback:** We generate meaningful feedback that is used by students to clarify, prioritize, and internalize their strategic efforts to learn. Feedback is meaningful to students when 1) it clarifies how their current evidence of learning relates to success criteria, 2) it informs their efforts to prioritize the use of specific strategies to improve, and 3) it is used to take action that helps them prioritize and internalize strategic efforts to learn.

- **Purposeful Teaching and Learning:** We establish a shared purpose for learning and use assessment evidence and success criteria to help students develop deep understanding. We plan courses, units, and lessons that purposefully align standards, learning goals, success criteria, and instructional strategies. We clearly, consistently, and concisely communicate to students what is most important to understand, and what it means to understand, so we can prioritize each student's efforts to learn.

- **Conditions for Responsive Learning:** Responsive teachers are pro-active in their efforts to use the right strategy, in the right way, and at the right time to support students' learning. Responsive learners believe the effective use of strategies is more important than their innate ability. Rather than being merely compliant, they prioritize their strategic efforts to develop a deeper understanding of content, concepts, and skills as aligned to shared success criteria. They are responsive to feedback that affirms and informs their strategic efforts to clarify misconceptions, improve important skills, learn new strategies, and overcome obstacles that impede their learning.

In the chapters that follow, each of these elements is further defined, relevant examples are shared and analyzed, and action steps are presented. Figure 3.2 summarizes these elements of clarity. This is a systemwide approach to minimizing clutter and creating clarity. Although many of the strategies described can be used at any time in any classroom, the full benefits are derived when each component—starting with establishing shared success criteria—are developed and used in concert with the other.

Figure 3.2

Elements of Clarity and Aligned Action Steps

Elements of Clarity	Action Steps
Focused Success Criteria	• Adopt a shared scale for success criteria across all disciplines. • Focus on a limited number of transferable priority standards in each discipline. • Align priority standards to our shared scale for success criteria. • Ensure success criteria for priority standards are published and accessible.
Intentional Assessment Design	• Establish a shared language of prioritized assessment terms. • Intentionally design assessment tasks to gather aligned evidence. • Intentionally minimize clutter from assessments.
Reliable Inferences	• Describe the quality of assessment evidence in terms of relevant success criteria. • Describe the depth of student understanding while accounting for the context of the assessment task. • Gather metacognitive evidence to make thinking skills observable. • Establish interrater reliability among teachers.
Meaningful Feedback	• Teach students to use feedback in meaningful ways. • Give meaningful judgmental feedback. • Give meaningful developmental feedback.
Shared Purpose	• Establish a shared purpose for learning in a standards-based system. • Align priorities for learning at the system, discipline, course, and unit levels. • Communicate your priorities and purpose clearly, concisely, and consistently.
Responsive Learning	• Develop students' ability to strategize by aligning instructional strategies and tasks to leaning goals and success criteria. • Develop students' ability to plan, monitor, and evaluate the relationship among effort, strategy, and results. • Protect students' ability to prioritize.

From Clutter to Clarity: Questions
for Discussion and Reflection

1. If you were to identify an APGAR equivalent for a subject you teach, what five skills would you include?

2. How do you currently use an assessment in your classroom to improve student learning? How do your students?

3. How analogous are the four hospital scenarios to situations you've seen in schools as a student, a parent, or an educator? What differences or similarities inform or affirm your thinking about how assessment information is, or should be, used in schools?

4. Review the six assessment components that create clarity for teaching. Which do you already do well as a school or district? Which might be an area of opportunity for creating clarity for learners?

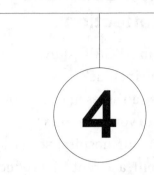

Focused Success Criteria

How do shared, focused success criteria minimize clutter and create clarity for teaching and learning? Consider the following scenarios.

Non-exemplar: All these kids care about are grades. Six teachers in a middle school's social studies department each assess students in very different ways. When students are given success criteria in the form of rubrics, the categories, descriptors, and scales vary from class to class and project to project. Students ask a lot of questions about their work, but the questions are usually about directions or how points are added to determine a grade. A student asks, "What do I need to do to get four points on this?" The teacher answers and then sighs. In her head, she thinks, "All these kids care about are grades."

Non-exemplar: You must plan common units and give common assessments. Teachers at an area high school are frustrated with their students' results on the state math assessment. Despite additional time working on basic algebra skills and the availability of new remedial courses, students don't seem to be making progress. The principal sends an email to all algebra teachers with the directive that "You must plan common units and give common assessments." For their part, the teachers decide to do a unit every two weeks: one lesson per day for eight days, a review day on the ninth day, and a test on the tenth day. All tests have 25 problems. To ensure there are no complaints about grading, all problems have a single, "correct" mathematical answer.

Exemplar: The kids are starting to notice! A middle school establishes a shared scale for high-quality work. The scale has four levels and progresses from basic skills and rote knowledge to fluent application of complex skills on open-ended tasks. Teams identify five to eight priority standards in each discipline. Some of the priority standards are even similar across disciplines. For example, the standard "supports claims with evidence" and the aligned descriptors read similarly in all four core academic subjects. Although the content changes from grade to grade and course to course, the expectations for quality are focused and consistent.

At a team meeting, Ms. Smith shares an anecdote from her math class. After class, a student comes up to her and says, "Mr. Johnson uses this rubric for 'supports claims with evidence' too, except you have us use math vocabulary and he has us use literature stuff."

"The kids are starting to notice!" Mr. Johnson replies. He continues, "We've got one agenda item today. How are we defining the difference between 'describe' as compared to 'explain' in our classes and what are some examples of quality descriptions and explanations we'll use as anchors to share with our students?"

Focused Success Criteria

Success criteria describe what evidence of understanding looks like. Success criteria are *focused* when they are aligned, systemwide, to a limited number of prioritized standards along a shared scale that describes what it means to understand. Shared success criteria focus teachers' and students' strategic efforts to make progress toward the most important skills and understandings in a discipline.

Why do we need to bother teaching your discipline? I ask teachers this question as a starting point for determining what is most important for students to understand in each discipline. I may hear slightly different details, but the essence of the replies is always the same: "We need students who can think like scientists/mathematicians/historians/writers/engineers/

artists/musicians/citizens who can work with others to solve problems that don't even exist yet."

This is a powerful response, and many noted researchers and learning theorists wholeheartedly agree:

> The curriculum of a subject should be determined by the most fundamental understanding that can be achieved of the underlying principles that give structure to a subject. (Bruner, 1960, p. 6)

> Students should probe with sufficient depth a manageable set of examples so they come to see how one thinks and acts in the manner of a scientist, a geometer, an artist, a historian. . . . The purpose of such immersion is not—I must stress—to make students miniature experts in a given discipline, but to enable them to draw on these modes of thinking . . . to understand their world. (Gardner, 2000, p. 118)

Teaching students to see a discipline as a way of understanding—rather than as a receptacle to store pieces of information they may find useful someday—requires us to focus our collective efforts on what matters most. If what we say matters most are all the facts and details in a discipline, there will always be too much content and not enough time. A more productive approach, as Bruner and Gardner remind us, is to focus on what it means to understand the underlying principles that give structure to a subject.

To identify these principles in a manner that brings focus to teaching and learning, I presented three questions in Chapter 1 that schools need to answer as related to what it means to understand, what is most important to understand, and how to prioritize students' strategic efforts to understand what is most important. Answering these questions is essential to transcending the scattered expectations that students experience as they move from course to course and classroom to classroom. To be able to develop systems-level answers to these questions, we need to begin with three slightly different questions to align and focus our expectations for evidence of understanding as aligned to our priorities:

- What does it mean to understand?
- What do we accept as evidence of understanding?
- What is most important to understand in a discipline?

What does it mean to understand?

Suppose I told you that a student scored 95 percent, or a 3.5/4.0, on two history assessments. Based on these scores, it is appropriate to infer that the student earned a high grade, but how well does this student understand the content, concepts, and skills taught in the unit? The inference you can make about student understanding varies dramatically depending on the rigor of what was measured and the expectations for quality.

Now consider what this score—from two different assessments in the same class—might mean. Assessment 1 required the student to identify the correct definitions of 20 basic vocabulary words. From this, I can interpret the grade to mean that the student knows most of the basic vocabulary in this unit. By contrast, Assessment 2 asked the student to engage in a complex set of skills that required him to make meaningful connections across discipline-specific concepts and generate a solution to a complex problem. From this, I can interpret the grade to mean a sophisticated understanding of content, concepts, and skills.

Unless we have a shared meaning of what it means to understand, numerical values can distort, or even wildly misrepresent, the meaning of assessment evidence as related to standards. To clarify the meaning of scores or grades, we need to first clarify what it means to understand. A taxonomy such as the Structure of the Observed Learning Outcome (SOLO) (Biggs & Collis, 1982, Biggs & Tang, 2011) can provide teachers and students with a shared language of what it means to understand along a reliable scale of increasing levels of depth or complexity. Other frameworks, such as Bloom's Taxonomy (see Anderson & Krathwohl, 2001), Webb's Depth of Knowledge (1997), or Marzano's general scale (2007), can also be adopted. What matters is that you select or develop a scale that articulates a valid, reliable sequence from more basic to more complex levels of skill and understanding. I've chosen to use SOLO in this book because I believe it is easiest to conceptualize.

Too often, taxonomies for learning are used as a shopping list to gather and place rigorous verbs into assessment tasks. More powerfully, a taxonomy can be used to develop and align standards, learning goals, assessment tasks, and success criteria. When used in these ways, they establish a set of shared constraints that align learning goals and assessment tasks, eliminate clutter, create clarity across units and programs, improve the reliability and accuracy of feedback and grades, and raise student achievement:

> When the aim of teaching is that students learn specific content to acceptable standards, aligning the assessment of learning to what is to be learned is not only logical, it is more effective in getting students to learn. Cohen (1987), after a comprehensive review, was so impressed that he called alignment between the assessment and the intended learning outcome the 'magic bullet' in increasing student performance. (Biggs & Tang, 2011, p. 98)

The SOLO taxonomy (Biggs & Collis, 1982) consists of two phases (quantitative and qualitative) and five levels of understanding (prestructural, unistructural, multistructural, relational, and extended abstract) that scaffold from basic awareness of content to sophisticated transfer (see Figure 4.1).

Figure 4.1

Structure of the Observed Learning Outcome

A general scale for categorizing complexity of learning goals and depth of understanding.			
Unistructural **Level 1**	**Multistructural** **Level 2**	**Relational** **Level 3**	**Extended Abstract** **Level 4**
I can define terms or follow simple procedures.	I can describe or combine terms and follow multistep procedures.	I can connect, compare, and explain relationships between content and concepts or strategically engage in complex procedures.	I can transfer skills and understandings to new topics, concepts, or contexts to engage in, and reflect upon my approach to strategizing and solving authentic, novel problems
Quantitative phase (acquiring knowledge and following steps in simple procedures)		Qualitative phase (deepening understanding through transfer and strategic application of complex procedures)	

Level 0 = Prestructural: "I haven't demonstrated evidence yet./This is new to me."
Note: Since the first level of understanding is an absence of awareness, it doesn't require descriptors.

Notice the distinction between the quantitative and qualitative phase:

- In the quantitative phase, knowledge is added. The learner is identifying or acquiring more content or can do more procedures, but it merely rests on the surface of the learner's existing ways of thinking and doing.
- In the qualitative phase, the learner is integrating and synthesizing content, concepts, and skills. At this level, the learner is developing a deeper awareness of how to transfer new ways of thinking and doing to see patterns and hypothesize solutions that were previously beyond his or her reach.

When a scale such as this is used as a framework to scaffold learners from a more basic to a more complex application and understanding of content, concepts, and skills, we can help clarify for students that understanding is not the same thing as rote application or retelling. Instead, this approach emphasizes what Jay McTighe (2014) describes as the goal of education: *transfer*. Transfer is what happens when a learner can apply the most important understandings in a discipline to new ways of thinking and new contexts.

What do we accept as evidence of understanding?

Too often, standards are viewed as a long checklist of isolated items that students should know and be able to do. If there are 180 days in a school year, by the end of a typical K–12 experience, students have had 2,340 lessons in each of the core subjects. To prioritize how that time is used, we have to begin with the end in mind. A curriculum that fails to prioritize how this time is spent will have little cumulative effect in its efforts to support deeper learning. A curriculum focused on ensuring students can internalize and transfer their learning to new contexts requires a clear focus of what is most important to understand and what it means to understand.

In *The Disciplined Mind*, Howard Gardner (2000) describes the importance and the challenges of teaching for understanding. He argues that perhaps the most important element is ensuring students have an appreciation for what will be accepted as evidence of understanding:

> Students must know what they have to do: they must be familiarized with the ways in which they will be asked to perform their understandings; and they must appreciate the criteria by which their performance will be judged. Far from being subjected to mysterious exams . . . students should be exposed from the beginning to performances reflecting various degrees of competence; they should be assured that they will have plenty of opportunities to practice the required performances and to secure helpful feedback; and they should be confident that the culminating performances will typically be occasions for pride, rather than for apprehension or shame. (p. 131)

What Gardner describes here is a system of assessment that is of a completely different order than the standardized tests, statewide proficiency tests, unit tests, or midterm exams that likely come to mind when students or noneducators think of assessments. Gardner's vision transcends the antagonistic view of assessment as something done *to* students and places the term in its historically accurate context: something we do *with* students.

When Gardner says students "must appreciate the criteria by which their performance will be judged" (2000, p. 131), he's not talking about ensuring they know specific project requirements, such as the size of the poster board to be used, the number of paragraphs to write, or the grading scale on which they'll be judged. Rather, he's talking about the importance of understanding the most important success criteria as a necessary condition for them to take an active role in their own learning.

Criteria are descriptors of evidence. Criteria are what make systems of reliable assessment possible. They place common parameters around everyone's answer to the question "What will we accept as evidence of success?" Most powerfully, success criteria are used by students to self-assess their current level of understanding and consider strategies to improve. Indeed, anyone who displays competence in any field has internalized—and is able to reflect on—the quality of their work as related to success criteria.

For example, suppose you call a contractor to repair some drywall in your house. The contractor has spent years honing his craft by pursuing skills related to the relevant criteria for quality. The success criteria can be expressed as a transferable standard for craftsmanship, such as "Fluently apply skills and resources to design and develop high-quality products with the craftsmanship, precision, and accuracy necessary to serve its intended and aesthetic purpose." This criterion is made observable by two pieces of evidence in this specific context:

- All surfaces, angles, and corners are smooth and flush with the existing wall.
- The finishing compound will have an identical texture as the existing surface.

The contractor may even put the success criteria and aligned evidence in a contract to ensure you are both on the same page regarding expected outcomes. These statements are examples of a prioritized standards area (craftsmanship) and aligned evidence (*smooth and flush, identical texture*). They articulate the transferable, relevant, observable attributes of a high-quality performance for a variety of similar tasks.

These criteria and evidence are identical to those that were used formatively as the contractor was learning his trade. When he started, maybe he didn't know what finishing compound or an aesthetic purpose were. Over time, and with experience, he learned the language of the craft, the skills of the craft, and the language of quality so he could engage in, and reflect on, his ability to transfer those skills to do work that was of high quality on increasingly complex tasks.

In Gardner's words, the contractor came to appreciate the success criteria by which his performance would be judged because he saw those elements as transferable, useful areas to focus effort and strategy to produce high-quality work.

This pathway to understanding can be articulated and aligned using the SOLO framework (see Figure 4.2). Notice the transferability of these success criteria. Vocabulary from a specific trade (drywall, masonry, wood working, 3D printing, sewing) could be used to identify the types of materials or the specific skills to be applied, but the most important attributes of craftsmanship are identical—and therefore transferable across hundreds of tasks in each of the trades.

Figure 4.2

Example of Transferable Success Criteria for a Standard for Craftsmanship

Craftsmanship: Fluently applies skills and resources to design and/or develop high-quality products with the craftsmanship, precision, and accuracy necessary to be useful for their intended purpose.			
Unistructural	**Multistructural**	**Relational**	**Extended Abstract**
Identifies necessary resources and materials to complete a project.	Uses resources and materials correctly to apply necessary skills to complete isolated tasks.	Fluently applies skills and resources to design and develop high-quality products with the craftsmanship, precision, and accuracy necessary for the product to serve its intended and aesthetic purpose.	Given a complex design task with process or product constraints, fluently applies skills and resources to design and develop high-quality products with the craftsmanship, precision, and accuracy necessary to serve its intended and aesthetic purpose.

This example shows how important, transferable elements in a discipline can be described using a scale that articulates depth of understanding as aligned to evidence of understanding. How can we identify the most important, transferable ways of thinking and doing in our own disciplines?

What is most important to understand in a discipline?

To prioritize students' strategic efforts to learn, we first need to focus their attention on the most important transferable standards in each discipline. For a powerful metaphor for understanding how we can prioritize our time and energy to focus on what's most important for our students to understand, consider the obstacles and opportunities we face when organizing physical space. In her book *The Art of Discarding,* Nagisa Tatsumi (2005) explains that prioritizing is a two-part process; it requires identifying what is most important and discarding the clutter. Unfortunately, people are remarkably adept at justifying why almost all their possessions are important and rationalizing why nothing can be eliminated. This failure to declutter comes at a cost. Unless we eliminate clutter, we can't focus on what is important because we spend too much time and energy sorting and sifting through things that aren't important.

Marie Kondo (2014) drew on Tatsumi's work to create her own method of identifying what is most important and decluttering. I've summarized some relevant portions of Kondo's strategies here:

1. Organizing and eliminating clutter takes time but pays off in the end.
2. Imagine your ideal space where you have more time and energy to focus on what is most important.
3. Ask yourself what is truly meaningful to you. What you prominently display should reflect what is most important.
4. Discard what is not important; don't hold onto things that aren't meaningful.
5. Tidy by category (clothes, books, papers, miscellaneous objects, mementos) rather than by room; put everything of a similar type in one place.
6. Tidy in order; first clothes, then books, then papers, then miscellaneous objects, until you get to sentimental items. By starting with the big stuff, you don't get lost in the details of the little stuff or the nostalgia of the deeply personal stuff.

A quick scan of Pinterest reveals that many teachers have taken Kondo's method to heart. It's easy to find photos of beautiful classroom spaces free of clutter and full of purpose. Consequently, students benefit from well-organized physical spaces that draw their attention to what is most important. However, to truly transform learning in our classrooms, what if we applied the same, focused approach to prioritizing and decluttering the avalanche of expectations, assignments, projects, materials, resources, rubrics, and assessments that cause clutter and distract our students' strategic efforts to learn?

When we organize school by content-driven units, daily assignments, and tests, students come to see the purpose of school as not much more than the rote completion of tasks. We can tell students what is important, but they won't *learn* what is most important if we simply fill their time sorting through tangential standards, surface-level recitation of trivial content, activities that are interesting but do not develop or reveal deeper understanding, and other curricular clutter. Just as Kondo explains that putting things away in bins and drawers creates the illusion of decluttering, filling rows and columns in gradebooks with dozens of tasks and points creates the illusion of understanding. In reality, the more content we cover doesn't necessarily result in more learning; instead, it's more likely to prevent students from investing effort in the deep learning that matters most.

The same principles that guide Kondo's and Tatsumi's prioritization of physical spaces can be used to prioritize and align curriculum, instruction, and assessment to what is most important to understand. Consider the following. To establish priorities and shared success criteria, we must

- Commit to identifying prioritized standards and establishing shared success criteria. This takes time but will pay off in the end.
- Imagine how our students will apply the most important skills and concepts in the future and strive for that level of authenticity in our course, unit, and lesson design.
- Ask ourselves, "What is most important in this discipline, and how can it be made accessible with enough frequency and focus that it is internalized by students?" (Don't ask, "What is all the stuff I can teach that students may find useful someday?")
- Discard the trivia and "busywork" that distracts students from prioritizing their strategic efforts to learn.
- Prioritize by transferable standards (e.g., makes arguments and claims, uses textual evidence, makes sense of problems) rather than by unit topic or project (e.g., the Civil War, a research paper, quadrilaterals) so students see coherence as you focus on transferring skills and understandings across units.
- Organize courses, units, and lessons by prioritized standards first, then by aligned shared success criteria, then by acceptable evidence, then by learning goals, then by aligned tasks and activities.

When we heed this advice, we can establish the constraints necessary for clearer focus and deeper intentionality to prioritize *our* strategic efforts to help students prioritize *their* strategic efforts toward what is most important to learn.

Focused Success Criteria: Action Steps

Focused success criteria minimize clutter and create clarity for teaching and learning. To establish focused success criteria, use the following action steps:

1. Adopt a shared scale for success criteria across all disciplines.
2. Focus on a limited number of transferable priority standards in each discipline.
3. Align priority standards to our shared scale for success criteria.
4. Ensure success criteria for priority standards are published and accessible.

Action Step 1

Adopt a shared scale for success criteria across all disciplines. A variety of taxonomies for learning were discussed earlier in this chapter. This book uses the SOLO Taxonomy (Biggs & Collis, 1982), but other valid, reliable scales have been developed and can be used. To those ends, this action step requires you to do your research on various taxonomies for learning, engage in a collaborative process to select one, and commit to using it. This activity is the catalyst that sparks the systems-level clarity for everything that follows.

Action Step 2

Focus on a limited number of transferable priority standards in each discipline. Several years ago, I was consulting in a district that was aligning standards to curriculum, instruction, and assessment pertinent to career and technical education. We pulled together the lead teachers in the areas of business, culinary arts, accounting, computer programming, automotive technology, computer aided design, engineering, and career planning. Each program had multiple courses, teachers would often teach across multiple programs, and students would take as many as 6–10 courses across three or more programs. As we reviewed the standards frameworks in each area, we found more than 120 different standards, 500 learning priorities, and 2,400 performance indicators. Everyone acknowledged that the department, and its programs, lacked focus.

To prioritize standards for the program, we used the following criteria:

- Identify or develop five to eight standards that are used most frequently as ways of making—and sharing—meaning.
- Identify, or establish categories for, the standards that focus on skills that are important and transferrable—in other words, those that occur frequently within a discipline and can be applied across lessons, units, courses, programs, and authentic settings.
- Verify the selected standards by asking this confirmatory question: "Have we identified the standards that describe the patterns of thought and action in this discipline that are used by practitioners to prioritize content, concepts, strategies, and skills?"

By applying these criteria across 120 standards, five priority standards were identified. Although the specific content, concepts, and skills varied across each of the career and technology programs, all curricula, instruction, success criteria, assessments, syllabi, program guides, learning goals, and reporting tools could now be aligned to just five "universal" priorities:

- **Employability:** Knows expectations for employment and anticipates, and proactively addresses, work-related challenges and opportunities.
- **Authentic Application of Disciplinary Content:** Demonstrates understanding of, and can apply, discipline-specific content and concepts in authentic contexts.
- **Problem Solving:** Describes problem, determines a preferred outcome, identifies available resources, implements an efficient and effective strategy, monitors progress toward the outcome, and modifies strategies as necessary to achieve desired results.
- **Communication:** Communicates clearly and coherently to develop or explain important ideas; organization, language, and style are appropriate for the task, purpose, or audience.
- **Skills, Products, and Craftsmanship:** Fluently applies skills and resources to design and/or develop high-quality products with the craftsmanship, precision, and accuracy necessary to be useful for their intended purpose.

This is not simply a clerical task that sits on the first page of a program overview that no one will ever read. In the same way that Virginia Apgar's assessment allowed hospitals around the world to align strategy to results by focusing on the five most important aspects of a newborn infant's health, these five standards became the priorities for focusing collective efforts to support each student's learning in the career and technology program.

By focusing on these prioritized standards, it clarified that the purpose of each class in the program was not to teach students how to bake a carrot cake, build a mousetrap car, or design a marketing plan for a new soda. The purpose, rather, was to help students transfer discipline-specific skills and language to understand the problem-solving process. *The activities aren't transferable, but the priority standards are.*

Sorting by priority standards—rather than by course content—allowed teachers to immediately see the clutter problem and acknowledge the clarity paradox in the existing program. They'd been so focused on the details of their individual courses, they'd never stepped back far enough to focus on the most fundamental understandings that gave structure to their department. Furthermore, they'd never been clear with students that these were the most important, transferable skills worth pursuing. Suddenly, the importance of questions that had never been asked were suddenly revealed: How do we teach *problem solving?* Is there a problem-solving process we should all be teaching? How is problem solving similar when cooking, writing computer code, or fixing a car, and how do we help our students see those patterns?

Most academic disciplines require teachers to do less synthesis to establish priority standards than in an area as broad as *Career and Technical Education.* Individual content areas typically have a relatively narrow set of practice or process standards, which include transferable skills such as "uses sources as the basis for evidence," "attends to precision," "develops and uses models," or "uses data to support conclusions." Unfortunately, many states' standards documents dedicate a few pages to these types of standards only to have them fade into the clutter of dozens—sometimes hundreds—of pages of content that follows.

In these areas, the challenge is to focus on only five to eight of these standards as a single set of shared constraints and to step away from the belief that knowledge of rote academic content is the most important component of the curriculum. The payoff from doing this is significant. By actually prioritizing around a shared set of standards, we can focus students' efforts to develop a deep understanding of a set of skills that can transfer across courses, units, and lessons. (See Figure 4.3.)

Figure 4.3

Transferable Standards That Could be Adopted as Priority Standards and Aligned to Shared Success Criteria

Science & Engineering (NGSS)	Mathematics (CCM)
• Asks questions (for science) and defines problems (for engineering) • Develops and uses models • Plans and carries out investigations • Analyzes and interprets data • Uses mathematical and computational thinking • Constructs explanations (for science) and designs solutions (for engineering) • Engages in arguments from evidence • Obtains, evaluates, and communicates information	• Makes sense of problems and perseveres in solving them • Reasons abstractly and quantitatively • Constructs viable arguments and critiques the reasoning of others • Models with mathematics • Uses appropriate tools strategically • Attends to precision • Looks for and makes use of structure • Looks for and expresses regularity in repeated reasoning
Social Studies (WDPI)	**Writing to Support Claims (CCW)**
• Constructs questions and initiates inquiry • Gathers and evaluates sources • Develops claims using evidence to support reasoning • Communicates and critiques conclusions	• Development of ideas, claims, and evidence • Organization of ideas and reasoning • Writes with clarity and coherence • Word choice and sentence fluency • Proper mechanics, punctuation, grammar
World Languages Standards (CDoE)	**Reading Informational Texts (CCR)**
• Interpretive communication • Interpersonal communication • Presentational communication • Cultural competence • Connections to other disciplines	• Determines central idea • Cites textual evidence to support analysis • Analyzes key details • Analyzes the writer's craft and structure of a text

NGSS = Next Generation Science Standards, CCM = Common Core Mathematics, CCW = Common Core Writing, CDoE = California Department of Education, WDPI = Wisconsin Department of Public Instruction, CCR = Common Core Reading

Looking at these priority standards reveals why they are so powerful; they describe how individuals in various disciplines apply, and make meaning of, content. Although the associated skills are the essence of each discipline, they are often buried under the clutter of endless academic content and ambiguous language that prevents students from being able to use them to prioritize their efforts to internalize these ways of thinking and doing. The limited number of standards establishes a powerful set of shared, prioritized constraints that minimize clutter so we can emphasize what is most important. Students internalize these priority standards when they are the collective focal point of our time and energy spent teaching and learning.

Action Step 3

Align priority standards to our shared scale for success criteria. By identifying and committing to a limited number of transferrable priority standards, teachers and students can more effectively see through the clutter and provide systems-level clarity for everyone in the school community about *what is most important to understand* in each discipline. Identifying a shared, general scale for success criteria—and aligning standards to it—helps further clarify and describe *what it means to understand* these priorities at different levels of depth and complexity. Now that we have these components in place, we can pull these two elements together to focus and align our collective efforts to support learning.

We can now take each standard and align it to our general scale to create aligned, shared success criteria. (See Figure 4.4 for an example.)

Figure 4.4

**Example of a Middle School Priority Standard
Aligned to a Shared Scale for Success Criteria**

Science 6–8: Engaging in Arguments from Evidence: Develops convincing arguments using evidence that supports or refutes claims for explanations, or solutions, about the natural and designed world.

Unistructural	Multistructural	Relational	Extended Abstract
Defines and identifies a claim, an argument, and specific evidence.	Describes each of the important elements of a claim, an argument, and specific evidence.	Given a claim, constructs an argument that supports or refutes the claim using aligned evidence and logical scientific reasoning.	Develops and supports a claim using relevant, well-chosen evidence and sound scientific reasoning as the basis for a well-constructed argument.

Alternatively, we can take a more conceptual standard and create aligned, shared success criteria using the same scale. (See Figure 4.5 for an example.)

Figure 4.5

Example of a High School Priority Standard Aligned to a Shared Scale for Success Criteria

Mathematics 9–12: Makes Sense of Problems: Approaches mathematical problems strategically and monitors progress toward a reasonable solution by determining what is to be solved for, what is known, what is not known, and identifying or modifying an efficient strategy to solve, and make meaning of, the problem.			
Unistructural	**Multistructural**	**Relational**	**Extended Abstract**
Identifies what is known and what one is trying to solve for in a given math problem.	Describes what is known, what is not known, and states what one is trying to solve for.	Selects and applies an efficient strategy that is useful to solve a problem based on what is known, not known, and what one is trying to solve for. If unsure, poses relevant clarifying questions.	Justifies an approach to solve a complex problem. Or, if unsure, explains what is not clear, what other strategies were tried, what specific clarifying questions were asked, how an approach was modified, or what resources were used to clarify next steps.

By articulating priority standards across a shared, common scale of success criteria, we can describe a clear, reliable path to describe what it means to understand what is most important. In the following chapters, I'll discuss how to develop and use these scales to create clarity and prioritize your development of curriculum, instruction, and assessment. Before we delve into those details, though, we need to clarify—for the entire school community—that these are our priorities.

Action Step 4

Ensure success criteria for priority standards are published and accessible. Once you've established priority standards and aligned them to a common scale for success criteria, they need to be published. This is no different from how the College Board shares its AP rubrics or how the International Baccalaureate Programme shares its IB rubrics with teachers and students. These programs are held in high esteem by colleges and universities around the world because they've articulated clear expectations for quality and rigor to guide teachers' and students' efforts to demonstrate evidence of learning.

Because these scales are the focal point of assessment, curriculum, goal setting, and grading, they should be omnipresent and used frequently and consistently. A scale for success criteria that is used only once is no more effective to improve one's learning than eating a single healthy meal is effective in improving one's health. Consider the example of how such a scale has been organized for a set of priority standards in science in Figure 4.6. The scale fits on a single sheet of paper and can be given directly to students to focus on what is most important to understand and what it means to understand as they set goals for learning, prepare for assessments, monitor their own progress, respond to feedback, and self-assess.

It's also important to present the shared success criteria in a common format. Regardless of the format you select, as long as you are using a valid, reliable scale, the shared formatting will create clarity and consistency for students. For example, you could list the priority standard areas in the first column and the scaled descriptors in the top row. Begin with the most basic descriptor of performance on the left and progress to the right with increased complexity. Every conceptual scale or descriptor in Western discourse (e.g., calendars, number lines, written text) moves from left to right. The path from basic to complex levels of understanding should be articulated no differently.

Focused Success Criteria: A Summary

By developing, publishing, and using priority standards aligned to a shared scale for success criteria, we establish a focus for our curriculum, instruction, and assessment. By identifying a manageable number of prioritized constraints, we can take steps to create clarity and alleviate the clarity paradox. We'll discuss more about how to communicate these elements clearly, consistently, and concisely across programs, courses, units, and lessons later in this book. For now, let's step back and acknowledge the power of these four action steps.

Figure 4.6

Shared Scale for Success Criteria Aligned to NGSS Science Practice Standards: Upper Elementary

	Unistructural	Multistructural	Relational	Extended Abstract
General Scale for Success Criteria	*I can define terms or follow simple procedures.*	*I can describe or combine terms and follow multistep procedures.*	*I can connect, compare, and explain relationships between content and concepts or strategically engage in complex procedures.*	*I can transfer skills and understandings to new topics, concepts, or contexts to engage in, and reflect on my approach to, strategizing and solving authentic, novel problems.*
Engages in Inquiry	Asks basic, descriptive, questions about observable evidence.	Asks questions about processes, events, or characteristics of objects in the natural world.	Asks specific, open-ended questions about form and function and/or cause-and-effect relationships between/among observable objects and unobservable phenomena.	Asks open-ended questions that can be investigated scientifically and/or used to determine or predict outcomes based on observation, evidence, and application of grade-level science concepts.
Develops and Uses Models and Drawings	Labels specific parts of others' models and drawings.	Replicates, labels, and describes others' models and drawings.	Makes and labels accurate models/drawings using grade-level science vocabulary that shows the relationships among variables/parts.	From one's own observations, develops, makes, and labels accurate models/drawings using complex grade-level science vocabulary to clearly show the relationships among variables/parts.
Carries Out Investigations	Identifies and follows individual steps in an investigation.	Follows steps and describes specific procedures in an investigation.	Explains and follows procedures and conducts investigations to gather relevant, accurate data using fair tests and appropriate measures.	Evaluates the appropriateness of, and makes recommendations to improve, procedures and measures in investigations to ensure they produce valid, relevant, accurate data.

	Unistructural	Multistructural	Relational	Extended Abstract
Analyzes and Interprets Data	Identifies and labels relevant data.	Describes relevant information as related to a specific argument.	Interprets data to accurately explain the evidence/results of an investigation or specific relationships among variables.	Analyzes and interprets data to draw relevant conclusions, make valid claims, or refine the design or use of a tool, process, or procedure.
Constructs Written Explanations	Applies basic vocabulary to identify scientific objects, processes, or events.	Describes relevant information as related to a specific argument.	Explains form and function, order, or cause and effect of scientific objects, processes, or events using specific details applied to grade-level vocabulary/concepts.	Justifies and supports explanations of scientific objects, processes, or events using specific evidence and relevant details consistent with scientific ideas, principles, and theories.
Uses Evidence to Support a Hypothesis or Argument	Identifies relevant information aligned to a specific topic.	Describes relevant information as related to a specific argument.	Explains how specific evidence supports or refutes a hypothesis/argument using grade-level science concepts.	Selects and uses evidence to clearly support or refute a hypothesis/argument based on complex grade-level science concepts.

- We've established a reliable scale to describe the characteristics of basic to complex evidence of understanding.
- We've established a shared vocabulary for what it means to understand. If a learning goal or assessment evidence is aligned to "level 3," whether that child is in 2nd or 11th grade, it means the student can *connect, compare, and explain relationships between content and concepts or strategically engage in the complex procedures* taught in the unit, quarter, or course.
- We've established a reliable scale to serve as a foundation for a reliable system of developing assessments, gathering evidence, giving feedback, and grading.

- We've established a manageable number of priority standards that identify the ways of thinking that can be transferred from lesson to lesson, unit to unit, and course to course.
- We've identified where teachers and students should focus their strategic efforts to learn.
- For a summary of important ideas and strategies discussed in this chapter, see Figure 4.7.

Focused Success Criteria: Revisiting the Scenarios

In the first scenario (All these kids care about are grades!), the teachers use different scales, point systems, and success criteria within the department. The clarity paradox and the clutter problem are both present. The success criteria and scales are arbitrary and do not align to shared expectations for understanding. Students see assignments as isolated, arbitrary, transactional tasks. Absent a clear understanding of what criteria for quality exist in the discipline, students focus their strategic efforts on accumulating arbitrary points.

In the second scenario (You must plan common units and give common assessments), the teachers alleviate the clarity problem by creating common assessments. However, because the teachers don't have a scale for success criteria that clarifies deeper levels of understanding, they've implemented a series of common assessments focused on surface-level knowledge. The principal's strategy rests on the premise that the teachers can improve student learning by aligning units to common assessments. However, rather than develop assessments that align expectations to the most important evidence of understanding at various levels of complexity, the teachers designed assessments that were easy to score.

In the third scenario (The kids are starting to notice!), the teachers effectively integrate each of the elements discussed in this chapter. They've created clarity for students by focusing their efforts on a manageable number of prioritized standards and aligned them to common, shared success criteria. Because of the prioritization and shared focus in each discipline, there are enough constraints that students can see—and transfer—important understandings across disciplines.

Focused Success Criteria: Questions for Discussion and Reflection

- What do we accept as evidence of understanding of the most important skills and understandings in our discipline?
- What are the most important understandings in our discipline?
- What are the priority standards in our discipline?
- How can we be clear about what high-quality work looks like as related to priority standards?
- If components described in this chapter were implemented in our school/district, how might teachers and students benefit after a few years of consistent effort to use them to prioritize students' strategic efforts to learn?

Figure 4.7

Focused Success Criteria: Avoiding Clutter, Minimizing the Clarity Paradox, and Choosing Clarity

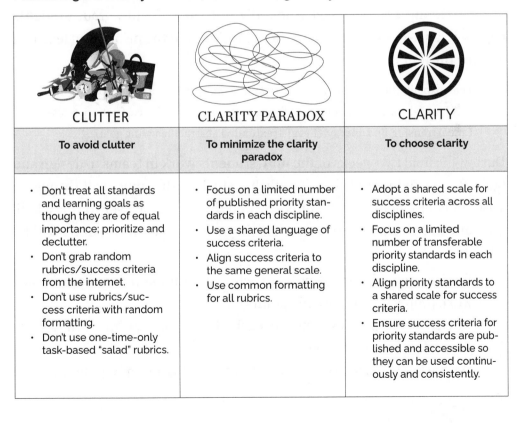

CLUTTER	CLARITY PARADOX	CLARITY
To avoid clutter	**To minimize the clarity paradox**	**To choose clarity**
• Don't treat all standards and learning goals as though they are of equal importance; prioritize and declutter. • Don't grab random rubrics/success criteria from the internet. • Don't use rubrics/success criteria with random formatting. • Don't use one-time-only task-based "salad" rubrics.	• Focus on a limited number of published priority standards in each discipline. • Use a shared language of success criteria. • Align success criteria to the same general scale. • Use common formatting for all rubrics.	• Adopt a shared scale for success criteria across all disciplines. • Focus on a limited number of transferable priority standards in each discipline. • Align priority standards to a shared scale for success criteria. • Ensure success criteria for priority standards are published and accessible so they can be used continuously and consistently.

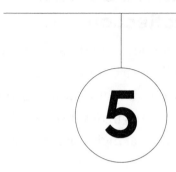

Intentional Assessment Design

How does the intentional design of assessment prompts and tasks minimize clutter and create clarity for teaching and learning? Consider the following scenarios.

Non-exemplar: We used a lot of duct tape. Eighth grade students engage in a six-week unit on Force and Motion, and the prioritized learning goal for the unit is

> I can explain the form and function of simple machines in a variety of specific, mechanical contexts as related to force, motion, mass, balance, friction, resistance, transfer, and energy. (Level 4, extended abstract learning goal)

During the final two weeks of the unit, students work in teams to design and build Rube Goldberg devices in which a steel marble must roll through a series of components until it flips a switch that causes a lever to ring a bell. Students are given a list of materials they can use and how points will be allocated:

- Device uses 2 levers (5 points each; 5 additional points each if they work properly = 20 possible points)
- Device uses 2 pulleys (5 points each; 5 additional points if they work properly = 20 possible points)
- Device has at least 2 ramps (5 points each; maximum 10 points)

- Device takes more than five seconds from marble drop until the bell (10 points per second = 50 possible points; no bell = no points)

On the day of the assessment, parents attend Rube Goldberg Day and see all the devices in action. Students bring their devices in and assemble them. The teacher, students, and parents move from station to station as teams of students drop their marbles and set their devices in motion. Only one group's device works perfectly and is given the maximum number of points. When the teacher asks those students to explain how their device worked, they look at one another sheepishly before one of them replies, "Sam had a really heavy marble and we used a lot of duct tape."

Exemplar: Establish defensible claims in history by acknowledging perspective. Mr. Jordan's U.S. history students are able to complete the first portion of their unit assessment on "Using Claims, Evidence, and Perspective to Understand the Great Depression" in about 10 minutes. This portion of the assessment includes a series of intentionally designed multiple choice and short fill-in-the-blank items aligned to one of the unit's learning goals: "Demonstrates knowledge of basic and more complex unit content."

For the second portion, students are given a performance assessment prompt and copies of two of their own formative assessments they completed earlier in the unit. One is a set of summary statements and examples students generated from a multiday lesson on "Establishing Defensible Claims in History: Acknowledging Perspective." The other includes written descriptions of how the Great Depression affected four fictional individuals who were used as cases throughout the unit to understand how events affected demographic groups differently.

The first two items on the second portion of the assessment require a written response and are aligned to one of the unit's learning goals: "Explains relationships among unit content and historical concepts." The final item requires students to transfer their understanding from the unit to new content. In this case, they need to interpret and analyze a political cartoon from the Great Depression they've never seen before. The task is designed to gather evidence aligned to the department's highest level of success criteria for "Interprets historical artifacts accurately from multiple perspectives."

Intentional Design

Intentionally designed assessment prompts and tasks gather specific evidence of student understanding as aligned to prioritized standards and success criteria. The design of a high-quality assessment requires us to focus on what content, concepts, and skills are most important—and eliminate the clutter of trivial content, random busywork, and other distractions. Intentional assessment design also requires us to pay attention to the specific language of assessment—words such as *explain, describe, demonstrate,* and *argue*—with the same level of attention to detail as is typically given to the academic content we teach.

Teachers and learners accept assessment as a part of how we do school. In its most traditional form, the teacher shares content and gives an assessment. The percentage of correct answers is then used to determine a grade. The measurement is efficient, objective, and precise. However, unless the assessment is a valid measure of the most important evidence as aligned to the most relevant success criteria, the measurement will be a wildly inaccurate indicator of the students' progress toward mastery of standards.

A "high-quality" assessment task is intentionally designed to help students produce the most important evidence of having achieved a learning goal as aligned to the most relevant success criteria. The task is a metaphorical bridge between the goal and the criteria. If that bridge doesn't connect these two components, it doesn't matter if the student walks across the bridge "correctly"; we can't make valid inferences about the student's ability to make it to the other side.

A "good" assessment gathers reliable evidence that can be used to make valid inferences about student learning. A basic understanding of the distinction between *validity* and *reliability*, and the important elements of each, provides an important foundation for intentional design of high-quality assessments.

A "valid" assessment item gathers evidence of what it is intended to measure. In a standards-based system, the intent of any item is to infer knowledge or understanding of a learning goal as aligned to a specific criterion. This is why a standards-based system is described as criterion referenced. A well-designed item allows for a valid inference about the quality of *that* evidence as related to *that* criterion. James Popham (2010) explains the essence of validity with the following adage: "Validity resides not in a test itself but, rather, applies to the accuracy of the inferences we base on students' tests performances" (p. 41).

With Popham's wisdom in mind, consider a simple math problem: *What is 3 + 8?* If we are trying to make an inference at a unistructural level, with a standards-aligned learning goal of "knows addition math facts in isolation," as aligned to success criteria along the lines of "with accuracy," then the item allows for a valid inference. However, if the standards-aligned learning goal was "adds multidigit numbers with decimals," then the item does not allow for a valid inference—even if the student answers the item accurately—because it won't produce evidence related to that specific learning goal.

Reliability is another critical component to understand when designing and interpreting the results of assessments. Reliability refers to the consistency with which an assessment measures what it is intended to measure. Just as a reliable thermometer will consistently give accurate information about the temperature outside, a reliable assessment will consistently give accurate information about a student's progress toward standards. However, the measurement tool must also be designed to allow for a valid inference of what it is intended to measure. No matter how reliable the thermometer is in measuring temperature accurately, it will not allow for a valid inference about the barometric pressure. Similarly, no matter how reliable an assessment task may be in gathering evidence of surface-level knowledge, it will not allow for a valid inference about deep understanding. Suppose students consistently average 95 percent on an assessment task every year in a science class. The assessment task is clearly reliable. However, if the task is a simple word search and is being used as evidence of students' deep understanding of science skills and concepts, it is invalid. It misrepresents students' true level of understanding.

We've already identified priority standards and aligned them to a valid, reliable scale of success criteria. Now we can focus our efforts on designing reliable assessment tasks that intentionally bridge the gap with evidence that allows for accurate inferences about students' progress toward standards. Consider these two items from an assessment on *Romeo and Juliet*. Which do you think is better?

- In what city do Romeo and Juliet live?
- If the play were only told from Romeo's perspective, what would be the most important difference in how the narrative is presented to the reader? State your claim and then use textual evidence to justify your response.

In workshops, I'll often ask a loaded question such as this. Teachers typically respond by saying, "The second one is better because it requires higher-order thinking." In truth, "better" presents a false choice. The quality of any assessment task can't be discerned by only looking at the item. We also need to know how it will bridge the learning goal to the success criteria.

To judge the quality of an assessment task, we need to know how the task aligns three design questions:

1. What are the relevant, shared success criteria?
2. What is the specific learning goal for which you want to gather evidence?
3. What prompt and task will require students to use the specific content or skills that will generate evidence of the learning goal as aligned to the specific success criteria?

We can now use these three questions to better discern the "quality" of our questions about *Romeo and Juliet*. Figure 5.1 reveals how these two items can each produce valid evidence at two different levels of understanding:

- One item is aligned to the unistructural level about a specific piece of textual evidence. The other is at the extended abstract level about deep understanding of how the writer's perspective affects the narrative and plot.

- Each item requires the student to produce observable evidence at a specific level of rigor as articulated in the success criteria.

Figure 5.1

Alignment of *Romeo and Juliet* Prompts and Tasks to Success Criteria for *Reading Key Ideas and Details*

	Unistructural	Multistructural	Relational	Extended Abstract
General Scale for Alignment of Success Criteria	*Defines terms or follows simple procedures.*	*Describes or combines terms and follows multistep procedures.*	*Connects, compares, and explains relationships between content and concepts or strategically engages in complex procedures.*	*Transfers skills and understandings to new topics, concepts, or contexts to engage in, and reflect upon, one's approach to strategizing and solving authentic, open-ended problems.*
Reading: Key Ideas and Details Scale for Success Criteria	Identifies and selects relevant details in a text.	Identifies and describes or classifies relevant details in a text.	Cites strong and thorough textual evidence to support accurate inferences and explanations to determine meaning of narratives or explain plot, setting, character, and theme.	Establishes, supports, or analyzes claims by citing strong and thorough textual evidence based on sound reasoning and justification within the text, across texts, or to the real world.
Alignment of Valid, Reliable Assessment Task	In what city do Romeo and Juliet live?	What are three pieces of textual evidence that show the tension between the Capulets and the Montagues? Give three quotes.	Select a quote that exemplifies the theme of love in the text. Explain what the quote means literally and how it relates to the theme.	If the play were only told from Romeo's perspective, what would be the most important difference in how the narrative is presented to the reader? State your claim and then use textual evidence to justify your response.

High-quality assessment items are intentionally designed to bridge standards-based learning goals to focused, standards-based success criteria. Aligning specific assessment items to specific levels of success criteria allows teachers to collect reliable evidence and make valid inferences about each student's progress toward standards (Figure 5.2).

Figure 5.2

Using SOLO to Intentionally Gather Assessment Evidence to Aligned Learning Goals and Success Criteria

	Unistructural	Multistructural	Relational	Extended Abstract
If general scale for success criteria are:	*I can define terms or follow simple procedures.*	*I can describe or combine terms and follow multi-step procedures.*	*I can connect, compare, and explain relationships between content and concepts or strategically engage in complex procedures.*	*I can transfer skills and understandings to new topics, concepts, or contexts to engage in, and reflect upon, my approach to strategizing and solving authentic, open-ended problems.*
Then examples of important terms in aligned learning goals are:	• memorize (in isolation) • identify (isolated parts) • define (basic) • recall • follow rote steps • restate (basic)	• memorize (among categories) • identify (characteristics) • define (complex) • re-state (complex) • describe • classify • follow multiple steps • organize	• compare and contrast • explain (known) • given claim/ evidence; argue • given framework; analyze • summarize • interpret meaning	On open-ended, authentic tasks: • design and justify/explain • determine and justify • hypothesize and justify/ explain • generate and explain • generate criteria and strategize • evaluate and explain

	Unistructural	Multistructural	Relational	Extended Abstract
Therefore, intentionally designed assessment tasks will provide evidence of:	• told • defined • "You gave and I solved" • "saw and did" • replicated • selected	• told more • "definitions/parts are" • "You gave and I solved more" • "saw and did more" • replicated more • described • organized • summarized parts	• Summarized/Identified/Applied/Synthesized and explained • Applied and explained/justified complex process • "Predicted what would" • Supported • Fluently/Efficiently/Strategically	On an open-ended, authentic task: • Hypothesized and supported/justified with evidence • Established criteria and supported/defended rationale • Defined parameters, designed solution, and explained rationale • Provided or developed specific examples that demonstrated general principles

Intentional design also requires us to think about how assessment tasks will help or hinder learners' efforts to produce evidence that represents their true level of understanding. Imagine trying to learn to drive a car with a manual transmission in a city you are visiting for the first time. The roads are hilly and narrow, it is nighttime, there is a lot of traffic, and your driving instructor is giving you a stream of directions in a language you don't know well. Performing any one of these tasks in isolation is challenging. But having to do them at the same time might cause you to simply pull over to the side of the road. When your brain is confronted with too much new information at once or too many distractions, the rational, defensive response is to shut down. John Sweller (2016) describes the relationship among the task, learner, and environment as *cognitive load.*

Suppose after you've pulled your car over, you switch positions and your driving instructor takes the wheel. You marvel as she not only navigates the complex terrain and challenging conditions but also does so while speaking on a cell phone and eating a sandwich. How can we describe the characteristics of the context and the individual to explain such dramatically different responses to the same task?

Cognitive load theory helps teachers confront a paradox of the human mind; namely, we have an unlimited capacity to hold onto information once it has been committed to our long-term memory, but we have an incredibly limited capacity to hold onto new information in our working memory. The New South Wales Department of Education (2017) suggests teachers can help students prioritize their efforts to learn by keeping the following two axioms in balance:

> When information is very complex or new, it is important that teachers reduce the load on students' working memories as much as possible to maximize learning. When information is easy for students to understand, teachers can gradually increase the complexity of the lesson to maximize students' learning. (p. 4)

As we help our students prioritize, we cannot control where they may be on their path toward proficiency. However, when designing assessment tasks, we have to be intentional about minimizing distractions and eliminating the clutter that may inadvertently overwhelm students and invalidate our efforts to gather valid evidence of their understanding.

Assessment tasks can be designed to more intentionally eliminate clutter by awareness of the three dimensions of cognitive load:

- *Intrinsic cognitive load* is the amount of effort the learner needs to put forth to engage in the task itself; this will vary by learner, depending on background knowledge and fluency with the topic and skill.
- *Germane cognitive load* includes those elements that focus the learner's attention and effort toward the most relevant aspects of learning.
- *Extraneous cognitive load* includes elements of the task that are not relevant. This is anything in the task that distracts the learner from focusing on important evidence or the relevant success criteria and instead draws their attention toward clutter.

By focusing our assessments on evidence that is aligned to priority standards and shared success criteria, we've already taken an important step to help students manage cognitive load. Now we need to ensure we've eliminated clutter from the assessment process itself. In the language of cognitive load theory, we want to design assessments that minimize the amount of extraneous load and emphasize germane load to ensure students can manage the intrinsic load. To do this, we need to be clear about what academic content is relevant (the prompt), what we are asking students to do (the task), and the task-specific logistics of how we are asking them to engage in the process (the directions). Attending to the cognitive load across all these components improves the clarity and quality of assessment items and tasks.

Intentional Design: Action Steps

Intentionally designed assessment prompts and tasks minimize clutter and create clarity for teaching and learning. To design high-quality assessments, use the following action steps:

1. Establish a shared language of prioritized assessment terms.
2. Intentionally design assessment tasks to gather aligned evidence.
3. Intentionally minimize clutter from assessments.

Action Step 1

Establish a shared language of prioritized assessment terms. Before students reply to an assessment prompt, they engage in an internal dialogue about the language in the prompt: "What is my teacher asking?" If a middle school student looks at an item that reads "Describe how setting and character were used by the author to develop the plot." they need to know the academic terms (*setting, character, author, plot*) and the assessment terms (*describe, develop*).

If we teach students academic terms but do not also teach assessment terms, students can't produce valid evidence of understanding. Unless students have been taught these words, they become extraneous load that students see as clutter. This is challenging because, as educators, we see assessment terms such as *describe* and *develop* so frequently that we forget our students might not know what they mean. There is a name for this phenomenon—*the curse of knowledge*—and it impedes teaching and learning all the time. Cognitive scientist Steven Pinker (2014) defines the curse of knowledge as "a difficulty in imagining what it is like for someone else not to know something that you know" (p. 59).

The curse of knowledge subverts our efforts to see our classrooms through our learners' eyes. For example, you may spend an entire unit teaching academic concepts such as *character, conflict,* and *plot,* but when it comes time to assess that content, your students might get tripped up on what you mean by *describe* and *develop.* Alternatively, what if the prompt read "Cite a relevant example from the story and explain your rationale." We can become so focused on teaching the story and doing a great job helping students understand character, conflict, and plot that we forget words like *describe, develop, relevant example, explain,* or *rationale* are also essential vocabulary students need to respond to the prompt. The curse of knowledge also applies to skills. We routinely underestimate how long it took us to learn a specific skill. Furthermore, once we've learned a skill, we are more likely to underestimate how long it will take others to learn the same skill.

To prioritize students' efforts to produce their best evidence of understanding, we need to be attuned to the importance of verbs that occur frequently in success criteria, learning goals, and assessment tasks. Figure 5.3 shows 60 terms that frequently appear in a variety of academic standards and curricular frameworks, which I've kept over the years. If every state-mandated standards document on the planet were to disappear tomorrow, these words would still be among the most important, transferrable terms for thinking, doing, creating, and innovating. Start with a list such as this, or do a word-count analysis of your own standards, learning goals, and success criteria. Then select a manageable number of terms that appear frequently (approximately 8–10 at the elementary level, 12–15 at the middle school level, and up to 20 at the high school level), and are worthy of systems-level clarity and shared meaning to minimize the cognitive load of assessment prompts, and improve the reliability of assessments across units, courses, and disciplines.

Once terms have been identified, they need to be defined. After they are defined, they can be broken down into specific attributes of quality and

Figure 5.3

Assessment Vocabulary That Appears Frequently in Standards, Rubrics, and Authentic Work/Life Tasks

accuracy	construct	determine	integrate	represent
analyze	contrast	develop	interpret	resolve
argument	craftsmanship	effect	justify	review
attribute	critique	effective	model	revise
cause	create	evaluate	narrative	solve
central/main idea	data	evidence	organize	source
claim	defend	explain	precise/precision	summarize
clear/clarity/clarify	define	examine	produce	support
compare	demonstrate	factor	quality	synthesize
component	describe	hypothesize	reasoning	utilize
conclusion	design	identify	relationship	valid
conduct	details/detailed	infer	relevant facts	verify

aligned to specific prompts (see Figure 5.4). These prompts can be used to scaffold students toward clearer, more strategic thinking and higher-quality responses to assessment prompts. This shared language of assessment and its aligned components should be publicly accessible and the focus of vocabulary lessons and aligned learning goals. When students have the opportunity to see the consistency and clarity that comes from shared expectations for how they respond to assessment tasks that use these terms, we help them manage their cognitive load and can more reliably assess their true depth of understanding of academic content.

Figure 5.4

Examples of Focus Terms: High School-Level Common Language of Assessment

If our shared definitions of prioritized assessment language are:	Then we need to teach students that high-quality responses include the following attributes:	Therefore, we intentionally scaffold with prompts such as:
analyze: to separate something into smaller parts so each part can be considered independently based on specific criteria	• Defines/describes what is to be analyzed. • Describes relevant components of what is to be analyzed. • States criteria for analysis. • Explains meaning or relevance of parts as related to categories and criteria.	• What are you analyzing? • What are the relevant components? • What are the criteria? • How do the parts meet/not meet the criteria?
define: to use known words and examples to explain the important, essential, or unique attributes of a term	• States term. • Describes category to which it belongs. • Describes relevant/important attributes. • Shares examples; clarifies with nonexamples.	• What are you defining? • What is it a type of? • What are the important attributes? • What is an example? What is a nonexample?
describe: to identify and articulate the most important, unique, or relevant attributes of an object, an event, an idea, or a phenomenon.	• States term and category to which it belongs. • States most relevant attributes. • Shares relevant details aligned to those components.	• What are you describing? • What are the most relevant categories? • What are the most relevant and interesting details, or unique attributes aligned to those categories?
evidence: to use facts to support or refute a claim	• States criteria. • States claim. • Describes or shows evidence. • Explains relevance of evidence as related to criteria and claim.	• What are the criteria for high-quality evidence? • What is your claim? • What is the evidence aligned to the claim? • How is the evidence relevant? • How does the evidence meet criteria for quality evidence?

If our shared definitions of prioritized assessment language are:	Then we need to teach students that high-quality responses include the following attributes:	Therefore, we intentionally scaffold with prompts such as:
explain: to identify and articulate the most important attributes of a process or phenomenon in a way that can be understood by others.	• States term, event, process, or phenomenon. • Describes relevant components. • Describes the temporal relationships (*first, next, then*). • Shares relevant examples. • Shares relevant details.	• What is the process or event you are explaining? • What are the main, or most relevant, components? • What is the order they occur(ed)? • What is a relevant example? • What are the important details?
summarize: to capture the most important elements or ideas of a text/event/media in as few words as possible	• States what is to be summarized. • Identifies important components. • States important elements or ideas in as few words as possible.	• What are you summarizing? • What are the most important components? • What are the most relevant steps/components? • How can they be stated concisely and accurately in as few words as possible?

Action Step 2

Intentionally design assessment tasks to gather aligned evidence. Once priority standards, shared success criteria, and a common language of assessment have been determined, those components can be used to write assessment items that intentionally gather evidence to bridge the gap between important learning goals and relevant levels of shared success criteria.

Drawing from the categories you've identified in your shared success criteria, determine which standard area and which level of rigor you want to gather evidence of. For example, perhaps you are teaching a unit in which you want students to demonstrate understanding aligned to the priority science standard "Develops and Uses Models." At this point in the unit, you want students to demonstrate understanding at the *relational* level. Looking at your shared success criteria, you see the descriptor at that level is written as follows:

> Develops, labels, and revises models to represent an observable scientific object or event to show, or clarify, physical or conceptual relationships among variables/parts. (relational)

Keep in mind that this action step does not ask you to *develop* relevant success criteria. By *identifying* success criteria that have already been established, we ensure we are gathering valid evidence aligned to our shared reliable scale for rigor. Next, we consider the most important academic content in the unit. A learning goal is derived by taking the targeted level of shared success criteria and rephrasing relevant portions to include specific academic content.

> **Shared Success Criteria:** Develops, labels, and revises models to represent an observable scientific object or event to show, or clarify, physical or conceptual relationships among variables/parts (relational level).

> **Unit Content:** water cycle, atmosphere, condensation, evaporation, precipitation, moisture

> **Aligned Learning Goal:** Develops and labels models to represent the water cycle to clarify important relationships among variables.

We can now intentionally design a prompt that will provide evidence of important unit content and skills that "bridge the gap" between the learning goal and success criteria. An aligned prompt that incorporates all these elements at the relational level might read as follows:

> This detailed model of the water cycle has 15 different labeled components and 20 arrows *(students are given a graphic of this model). On the blank model (students are given an identical model but with no labels or arrows),* use only five elements and no more than five arrows to show the most important components of the system. Label each component, label each arrow, and explain why you think they are most important.

Remember, a "good" assessment item intentionally gathers specific, observable evidence aligned to a specific level of success criteria. Surface-level learning goals and success criteria discern if students are accurately acquiring content knowledge and lend themselves to short-answer, multiple-choice, matching, or routine mathematics problems. By contrast, deep understanding requires a more complex set of tasks to determine if students are integrating content, concepts, and skills into more sophisticated ways of thinking and doing. Gathering this evidence requires open-ended, extended-response, and multistep authentic problems.

The row labeled "Aligned Tasks" in Figure 5.5 shows examples of prompts for intentionally designed tasks aligned to each level of success criteria for the priority standards area "Develops and Uses Models" in science. Notice that these tasks don't reference any specific academic content; they are transferable and should occur frequently across units and courses. The bottom row shows how those tasks could be aligned to prompts in a specific unit—*Modeling a Process: Understanding the Water Cycle*. Be clear with students that the content may change between units, but the types of assessment tasks used to gather valid, aligned evidence are remarkably stable and can be used to prioritize their efforts to develop transferable skills and understandings across units and courses.

To intentionally gather evidence aligned to the unistructural level:

If the success criteria are at the unistructural level . . . the learning goal and aligned success criteria should state that the student is familiar with, or knows, specific academic terms or can follow isolated steps in a stated procedure.

Then an aligned assessment task will gather valid evidence if . . . the content is directly aligned to the standards and a specific unistructural learning goal. The items may be multiple choice, a short written response, a short written solution, or fill-in-the-blank:

- Which of the following is an example of a sedimentary rock?
- $50 \times 7 =$

To intentionally gather evidence aligned to the multistructural level:

If the success criteria are at the multistructural level . . . the learning goal and aligned success criteria should state that the student can describe elements or parts of specific events, systems, or principles or can follow specific, multistep procedures.

Figure 5.5

Example: Developing and Using Models in Science

Alignment of Proficiency Scale, Success Criteria, Learning Goals, and Sample Assessment Tasks				
	Unistructural	Multistructural	Relational	Extended Abstract
General Scale for Alignment of Success Criteria	I can define terms or follow simple procedures.	I can describe or combine terms and follow multi-step procedures.	I can connect, compare, and explain relationships between content and concepts or strategically engage in complex procedures.	I can transfer skills and understandings to new topics, concepts, or contexts to engage in, and reflect on, my approach to strategizing and solving authentic, open-ended problems.
Develops and Uses Models: Scale for Success Criteria	Identifies specific, relevant parts in a given model.	Identifies and describes specific, relevant parts of an object, an event, a process, or a phenomenon as represented in a model.	Develops, labels, and revises models to represent an observable scientific object or event to show, or clarify, physical or conceptual relationships among variables/parts.	Develops, labels, and revises models to represent, describe, and test observable and unobservable scientific phenomenon to show, clarify, or predict physical or conceptual relationships among variables/parts.
Aligned Tasks: Develops and Uses Models	Using a model . . . • Identifies specific, labeled parts. • Re-creates (copies) parts of an existing model.	Using a model . . . • Describes parts of an object or natural event. • Describes sequence of events or process of a scientific phenomenon. • Describes relevance or function of components.	• Develops and labels (not copies) a model that represents a scientific object. • Develops and labels a model that shows physical relationships among parts of a scientific object. • Revises a model given new information or to make it clearer.	• Creates (not copies) and labels a model to represent an observed scientific process or phenomenon. • Develops and labels a model to make inferences about steps in a process. • Develops and labels a model to show inferences about cause-effect relationships.

	Unistructural	Multistructural	Relational	Extended Abstract
Example Prompts & Tasks for Developing Models from a Unit on the Water Cycle	• Circle where evaporation occurs in the water cycle. • Re-create the picture of the water cycle from the textbook.	• Given a model of the water cycle, complete the following statements: First … then … next … finally …. • Given a model of the water cycle, label and then add a one-sentence descriptor for the areas where precipitation, condensation, and sublimation would occur.	• Given a detailed model of the water cycle that includes 15 different elements and 20 arrows, re-create the model using only five elements and no more than five arrows to show the most important components of the system. • Label each element and each arrow, and in a short paragraph, explain why the identified elements are most important.	• Look at the detailed model of the water cycle and read the short paragraph about how the water cycle normally works. Then, use your understanding of the water cycle to create and label a comparative model titled "Why Drought Cycles are hard to Break." Justify your rationale in a short paragraph that explains your model.

Then an aligned assessment task will gather valid evidence at that level of understanding if… the content is directly aligned to the standards and a specific multistructural learning goal. The items are typically multiple choice, matching, fill-in-the-blank, or a short written response:

- Which of the following are three characteristics of sedimentary rock?
- What is the value of x in the equation $7(4x) = 28$

To intentionally gather evidence aligned to the relational/extended abstract levels:

If the success criteria are at the relational/extended abstract levels … the learning goal and aligned success criteria should state that the student can explain relationships between specific content and concepts or strategically engage in specific complex procedures. At the extended abstract level, the learning goal and aligned success criteria should state that the student can transfer specific skills and understandings to new topics, concepts, or contexts to engage in, and reflect on, an approach to strategizing and solving specific, authentic, open-ended problems.

Then an aligned assessment task will gather valid evidence at that level of understanding if . . . the content and skills are aligned to the standards and specific learning goal but may require students to make inferences about similar content or analogous situations. The items typically require a longer constructed response, simulation, performance assessment, or other project.

- What is the most important difference in how sedimentary, as compared to igneous, rocks are formed? State your claim and then explain your answer. *(relational)*
- Jamal looks at the equation $7(4x) - 2 = 8(16) - 2$ and says, "By estimating, I can see that x must be greater than 4." What do you think led Jamal to that conclusion? Is he correct? In your answer, use the terms *estimate, order of operations,* and *equivalent. (extended abstract)*

Action Step 3

Intentionally minimize clutter from assessments. Intentionally designed assessment tasks help students prioritize their efforts to demonstrate understanding. Students need to know the most important attributes of quality (success criteria), what academic content is relevant (the prompt), what we are asking students to do (the task), and the specific logistics of how we are asking them to engage in the process (the directions). When these elements are intentionally aligned, we help students maximize the relationship between intrinsic load and germane load. When they are misaligned or unclear, the extrinsic load can distract students and invalidate the evidence.

The prompt is typically presented as a question, such as *Who was . . . ? Where did . . . ? What is . . . ? What might . . . ? How might . . . ? Why would . . . ?* or *When does . . . ?* It should be concise, clear, and closed-ended if assessing for surface knowledge. When gathering evidence of deep understanding, the prompt is open-ended (using words such as *explain, synthesize, develop,* or *hypothesize*) and typically requires an additional element of reflection or justification (e.g., *What led you to this conclusion? How would you modify your response?*)

The task describes how students will make their evidence observable. It should clarify how the evidence will be presented (e.g., in a written response, on a discussion board, in a presentation, in a diagram, in a piece of art, using a list of materials for a science investigation). It may specify required academic content (e.g., "Include the terms *mean, median, mode,* and *distribution* in your explanation").

Directions should be as clear, concise, and specific as possible to protect students' ability to prioritize their strategic efforts. They may include specific steps that must be done to complete the task, specific resources that must be used, and due dates. The directions might be integrated into the task to establish parameters around the final task. Parameters might include directions related to minimal components to ensure there is enough evidence (requirements such as *in a paragraph, a two-minute presentation, at least one quote,* or *a report with at least three data points*). Alternatively, parameters may include directions that establish constraints to ensure clarity and focus (by including requirements such as *in 200 words or less* or *without using a calculator*). Directions and parameters are an essential part of intentionally designed assessment items, but it is critical to note that they are *not* success criteria.

The ability to follow directions or adhere to parameters is evidence of following directions—not attaining learning goals When giving directions, avoid making them the focus of the assessment process. Too many steps, required details, or options add extraneous cognitive load that scatter—rather than focus—students' attention on the standards-related components of the prompt and the task. Always use directions and parameters to break tasks into smaller, more manageable pieces to ensure the student can focus on producing high-quality work.

When designing assessments, think about students' cognitive load and strive for balance among the prompt, task, and directions. The goal should always be to emphasize the germane portions and eliminate the extraneous ones in order to help learners manage their intrinsic load.

Consider the two assessment tasks in Figure 5.6. Even though both examples share the same learning goals and prompt, there are important differences in how the intentionality of the tasks and directions result in clutter or clarity.

Figure 5.6

Comparison of How Assessment Tasks Can Be Designed to Manage Cognitive Load

Learning Goals:
- Develops, presents, and supports a valid claim based on well-chosen, relevant, primary-source historical evidence. *(Aligned to level 4 for "Uses Evidence to Support Claims.")*
- Makes accurate, relevant connections to explain historical content, concepts, and chronology of events. *(Aligned to level 3 for "Written Explanations.")*

Prompt:
Was the 1950s defined primarily by conformity or rebellion? Support your claim with evidence and sound reasoning.

Non-Exemplar	Exemplar
Sample performance task with low germane load and high extraneous load	*Sample performance task with high germane load and low extraneous load*
Task and Directions: • Use at least five documents in your response from five different high-quality sources on the internet in a five-paragraph essay. • For prewriting and drafting, use the Smith College, Jones College, or Super Writers website for ideas for drafting and refining. Drafts due Friday. • After writing your five-paragraph response, create a slide show with a minimum of 10 slides, 10 different transitions, and 10 images. Presentations due next Wednesday. • Share your five-minute oral presentation in class next Wednesday, Thursday, or Friday. **Success Criteria:** • Five documents as sources • Well-written five-paragraph essay • High-quality slide show with 10 slides • Informative five-minute presentation	**Task:** Make and support a claim based on the prompt in a one-paragraph essay that focuses on either a political or cultural factor. Textual evidence will be drawn from any 3 of the 10 single-page documents/artifacts that have been provided. **Directions:** • **Step 1—Define Terms, Determine Sources, Draft Claim:** Define *conformity* and *rebellion*, select factor, draft a one-sentence claim, and make a list of three most relevant pieces of evidence. Due Tuesday for small-group discussion. • **Step 2—Draft and Self-Assess:** Draft a one-paragraph essay and self-assess your draft based on CER rubric. Due Thursday for small-group sharing and feedback. • **Step 3—Final Draft and Feedback:** Revise your draft using the self-reflection and self-assessment criteria. Due Friday; developmental feedback returned Monday with time in class to start edits and revisions. • **Step 4—Publish and Reflect:** Complete paragraph and reflection statement. Due next Tuesday. We'll do small-group read-alouds and write synthesis statements Tuesday in class. **Success Criteria:** Claim, Evidence, Reasoning (CER) based on descriptors in shared success criteria (used department-wide).

The non-exemplar lacks intentionality. Don't mistake its brief description of the task or minimal directions as evidence of low cognitive load. Because the tasks and directions are arbitrary and irrelevant to the learning goals, there is a high extraneous load. It exemplifies what *not* to do:

- Don't confuse the act of adding more tasks with increasing evidence of students' depth of understanding.
- Don't give tasks that have a high intrinsic load *and* high extraneous load (e.g., write multiple paragraphs, find sources, create a slide show, give a presentation) that you haven't already taught or for which you don't have evidence that students already know how to do.
- Don't give tasks that have a high intrinsic load (e.g., write a five-paragraph essay) without any opportunity for meaningful feedback about the initial elements (identify sources, establish a claim, establish supports for the claim).
- Don't give complex tasks that are a prerequisite for the most important work (e.g., find five primary sources online, yet the learning goal is related to writing and supporting valid claims).
- Don't confuse quantitative evidence (e.g., 5 paragraphs, 5 sources, 10 slides, 5-minute presentation) with evidence of a high-quality performance.
- Don't use valuable class time for tasks that have a low intrinsic load, low germane load, and high extraneous load (e.g., three days of students watching other students' presentations).
- Don't give vague success criteria (e.g., a well-written essay, an effective slide show, an informative presentation).

By contrast, the exemplar in Figure 5.6 uses the prompt, task, and directions to scaffold students toward evidence that meets the success criteria. Each step in the process is germane to improving the most important attributes of the assessment evidence. To ensure clarity:

- Use the tasks and directions to intentionally scaffold students from basic tasks (define terms, select factor, identify sources) to more complex tasks (establish a claim and support your reasoning).

- Give students the resources they need to eliminate the extraneous load of making them do it on their own (unless you are engaged in a learning goal for conducting research). If *selects, identifies,* or *chooses* is in the success criteria, give students more resources than necessary and require them to justify their choices.
- Ensure the prompt, task, and directions all have a high intrinsic load and germane load; this will support students' strategic efforts to think deeply about the process of developing high-quality assessment evidence that is aligned to the shared success criteria.
- Use tasks with focused constraints (e.g., choose three sources, choose between two factors, write one paragraph) to reduce extraneous load, but do not confuse the act of following directions or steps with evidence of understanding, or attaining, the transferable success criteria.
- Intentionally scaffold prompts across a series of smaller tasks to give students the opportunity to receive feedback as they plan, develop, and revise their assessment evidence.
- Teach students to use the shared success criteria as the basis for planning, developing, revising, and reflecting on the quality of their evidence.

Strategies to be supportive of students' cognitive load are described in Figure 5.7.

Intentionally designed assessment prompts and tasks allow teachers to gather the most important evidence of student understanding as aligned to the most relevant success criteria. The design of a high-quality assessment requires us to focus on what content, concepts, and skills are most important and eliminate irrelevant clutter—so students can prioritize their strategic efforts to demonstrate evidence of what they have learned. For a summary of important ideas and strategies discussed in this chapter, see Figure 5.8.

Intentional Design: Revisiting the Scenarios

In the first scenario (We used a lot of duct tape), there are serious alignment issues due to unintentional assessment design. It begins with a clearly articulated standard related to "the form and function of simple machines in a variety of specific, mechanical contexts as related to force, motion, mass,

Figure 5.7

Use Cognitive Load Theory to Intentionally Prioritize Students' Strategic Efforts to Develop Quality Assessment Evidence

To minimize extraneous cognitive load:	To build students' capacity to manage intrinsic cognitive load:	To maximize germane load:
• Ensure success criteria focus on the transferable attributes of the standards, and not elements of the task or directions that are arbitrary or irrelevant for future performances. • Minimize prompts and tasks that require students to interact with new content, new concepts, and new skills concurrently. • Avoid tasks that require a lot of time and materials but have little to do with evidence of understanding. • Don't confuse adding *more work* with developing *better evidence*. • Don't give tasks that divide students' attention among too many sources/resources.	• Scaffold assessment tasks from more basic to more complex levels of understanding. • Use priority standards and shared success criteria frequently to help students build familiarity of, and fluency in, the most important skills and understandings. • Use a shared language of assessment for words such as *explain, define, and describe*. • Give students time and teach them strategies (e.g., graphic organizers, outlines, prewriting) to plan their work. • Build opportunities for goal setting, self-assessment, and self-reflection before, during, and after the assessment process. • Allow students to use formative work—graphic organizers, notes, summary statements—when engaging in extended-abstract tasks. • Use a predictable format or "operating system" for course, unit, and lesson overviews.	• Align prompts and tasks to prioritized standards and shared success criteria. • Align prompts and tasks to the most important content, concepts, and skills. • Break complex tasks into smaller tasks that scaffold toward deeper learning. • Use directions to draw students' attention to the most important evidence in the most relevant, important success criteria. • Be specific. If you want students to use specific terms in an extended-abstract response, say something like "Use and underline the words *republic, democracy, representation,* and *proportionality* in your answer." • Give students specific, relevant resources rather than directing them to find them on their own.

balance, friction, resistance, transfer, and energy." Although the activity is hands-on, engaging, and incorporates elements of engineering and craftsmanship, there is nothing in the design of the task that gathers any evidence of students' understanding of force and motion. For the highest scoring group, their articulated evidence of understanding was the marble and the duct tape, which has nothing to do with standards-aligned success criteria. Due to the high extraneous load of the task and arbitrary success criteria, there is no aligned evidence to bridge the prioritized standard and the articulated success criteria.

The second scenario (Establish defensible claims in history by acknowledging perspective) intentionally draws on specific content and skills to scaffold from evidence of surface-level knowledge to evidence of deep understanding. The title of the unit even speaks to both the content and skills that are the purpose of the unit. The success criteria for developing and supporting claims are one of five priority standards used throughout the curriculum. The first portion of the assessment is closed-book/no resources because the purpose of that portion of the assessment is to see if students know the unistructural and multistructural academic content. Even though the questions are surface-level, they are framed in the context of claims—the specific skill that focused the unit. In the second portion of the assessment, students are given some of their formative work to use as a resource—just as adults do in the real world. The answers aren't "in" the resources, but they provide relevant information about the most important skills and some specific details required to complete the higher-level tasks so students can focus on what matters most—demonstrating understanding of the content at a deep level.

Intentional Design: Questions for Discussion and Reflection

- What is our shared language of the meaning of important assessment terms (e.g., *describe, explain, summarize, synthesize, justify*)?
- How do we use our scale of success criteria to develop valid assessment items?
- How do we minimize clutter in assessment tasks to help students focus on the most important evidence of understanding?
- If components described in this chapter were implemented in our school/district, how might teachers and students benefit after a few years of consistent effort to use them to prioritize students' strategic efforts to learn?

Figure 5.8

Intentional Design: Avoiding Clutter, Minimizing the Clarity Paradox, and Choosing Clarity

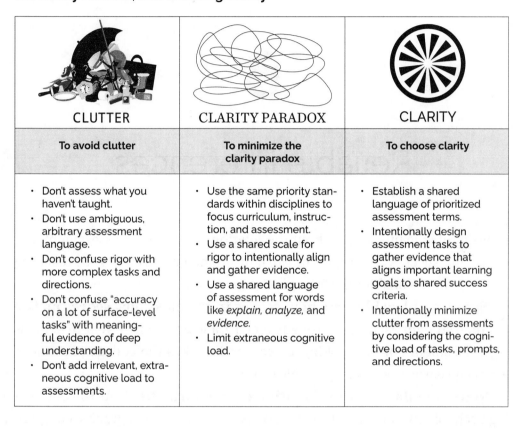

CLUTTER	CLARITY PARADOX	CLARITY
To avoid clutter	**To minimize the clarity paradox**	**To choose clarity**
• Don't assess what you haven't taught. • Don't use ambiguous, arbitrary assessment language. • Don't confuse rigor with more complex tasks and directions. • Don't confuse "accuracy on a lot of surface-level tasks" with meaningful evidence of deep understanding. • Don't add irrelevant, extraneous cognitive load to assessments.	• Use the same priority standards within disciplines to focus curriculum, instruction, and assessment. • Use a shared scale for rigor to intentionally align and gather evidence. • Use a shared language of assessment for words like *explain, analyze,* and *evidence.* • Limit extraneous cognitive load.	• Establish a shared language of prioritized assessment terms. • Intentionally design assessment tasks to gather evidence that aligns important learning goals to shared success criteria. • Intentionally minimize clutter from assessments by considering the cognitive load of tasks, prompts, and directions.

6

Reliable Inferences

How do reliable inferences about the relationship between assessment evidence and success criteria minimize clutter and create clarity for teaching and learning? Consider the following scenarios.

Non-exemplar: She gets high scores in the class; low scores on the exam. A student earns all *A*s (or advanced grades) the entire year in her college placement course. In May, however, she takes the college placement exam and earns the lowest possible score.

Non-exemplar: Is it explanation or memorization? At the end of a high school physics unit, students are asked, "In two paragraphs, compare and contrast three ways Newtonian mechanics and quantum mechanics are similar and three ways they are different. Provide a real-world example of both types." Most students give verbatim responses from class notes about three ways they are similar and three ways they are different, and all students provide the same example given by the teacher in class. The teacher scores each of the answers as a 4, which indicates "Student demonstrates deep understanding of complex content."

Exemplar: We agree what quality looks like. Teams of teachers at an elementary school have two professional development days each year to team score math and writing performance assessments. The teams select two priority standards in math and two in writing and build two different performance assessments to gather evidence at each level of their shared success criteria. After they administer the assessments, they reconvene to collabora-tively score student work samples. First, they identify anchor papers at each level of evidence. Then they break into pairs and score the assessments on each standard. If there is a discrepancy in scoring, a third scorer reads the work sample. (A third scorer is rarely necessary because after calibration, both scorers determine the same score 95 percent of the time.) By the end of the session, the teachers identify patterns of strength and challenge in stu-dents' work to guide their teaching in the coming months.

Reliable Inferences

An inference is a rational explanation and description of evidence based on an observation. As teachers, we spend a tremendous amount of time mak-ing inferences about the quality of students' work. We do this any time we describe how assessment evidence does, or does not, meet expectations for work that is of high quality. Someone who can consistently and accurately describe and explain how the most important evidence aligns to the most relevant criteria is a reliable assessor. Our ability to make reliable inferences about both the quality of the evidence and the depth of learners' under-standing are essential to prioritize our students' strategic efforts to learn.

"What was my score on the test?" is a question students ask all the time. On its surface, it's a simple question. Perhaps you add up the number of cor-rect items and divide them by the total, or maybe you add the points from several categories on a rubric. The result is a precise answer to the student's question: "You got a 91 percent" or "You got 17 out of 20." However, without a shared understanding of what the assessment evidence means as related to the most important success criteria, that "precise answer" may be an inac-curate representation of the quality of work or the depth of the student's understanding. This problem is not new. More than 100 years of educational research has shown that grades are unreliable (Guskey & Brookhart, 2019).

To this end, let's set the question about "my score" aside and reframe the question in terms of importance, validity, and reliability. An extremely savvy student might ask the question this way: "How would you describe the quality of my most important assessment evidence as related to the most relevant success criteria?" To make an accurate, reliable inference about the student's work, you would need to ensure that

- The success criteria are focused on the most important standards, represent the most important attributes of quality, and are arranged on a reliable scale. (See Chapter 4.)
- The prompt or task has been intentionally designed to reliably elicit valid, observable evidence of the prioritized standard as aligned to specific success criteria. (See Chapter 5.)
- The assessor is accurate and reliable and can consistently make valid inferences about the quality of the most important evidence as related to the most relevant success criteria.

We've already addressed the first two elements. Now we turn our attention to the process of using assessment evidence as the basis for valid, reliable inferences about the quality of students' work and their depth of understanding. The implications of aligning, or misaligning, these elements are profound. If students don't have an accurate understanding of how their assessment evidence relates to important success criteria, or if they believe success criteria are arbitrary because it depends on which teacher is looking at their work, how can they prioritize their efforts to learn? To ensure our inferences are accurate and consistent, we first need to clarify three questions:

- What is a valid inference?
- What is a reliable inference?
- Why is it essential that success criteria describe the most important assessment evidence?

What is a valid inference? A valid inference is an accurate conclusion about the quality of assessment evidence. A valid inference is possible when we base our conclusions on the most important assessment evidence as related to the most relevant success criteria.

What is a reliable inference? A reliable inference is consistently accurate. When a group of teachers can make consistent, accurate inferences about the relationship between the most important evidence and the most relevant success criteria when looking at samples of student work, they have a high level of what is called *interrater reliability.*

Why is it essential that success criteria describe the most important assessment evidence? The descriptors for valid and reliable inferences clarify why it is so important to establish success criteria that are focused on the most important, transferable attributes of quality in each academic area. Even with a well-designed task and prompt, invalid success criteria will always result in invalid inferences about the quality of student work and render subsequent communication about the quality of the evidence and the depth of the students' understanding meaningless. For example, task-based success criteria (e.g., five sentences, six presentation slides, three sources) are easy to score and are, therefore, highly reliable. But inferences about the quality of students' work will be invalid because the success criteria fail to describe important, transferable evidence of learning.

To see why transferable attributes of high-quality work, rather than task-based elements, are essential for establishing success criteria, look at the task, prompt, and rubric in Figure 6.1. Then consider the quality of the evidence in the two writing samples that follow. I've written the first sample myself under a pen name to mimic the type of writing that is common when students use task-based success criteria as a roadmap to accumulate points. The second writing sample is a seminal historical document written by Abraham Lincoln, which exemplifies transferable attributes of high-quality writing. Based on the success criteria in the rubric, the accurate, reliable scores for both essays are presented after each essay.

"The Civil War That Tore? Battles More Than Four" by Iman A. Student

There were at least four battles fought in the Civil War. Each of these battles has been documented by historians. The Battle at Fort Sumter started April 12, 1861. The Battle of Bull Run was July 21, 1861. The Battle of Shiloh started April 6, 1862. The Battle at Antietam was September 17, 1862. The Battle of Fredericksburg was December 13, 1862. The Battle of Gettysburg started July 1, 1863. In addition to the details of name, month, date, and year, there are more details. Another detail about these battles is that they were all important enough to be seen as major battles nearly 150 years later. These battles were important. These battles cost thousands their lives. These battles are documented in old photographs and in museums. I've supported my claim with evidence and given details on six examples. As you can see, there were at least four battles in the Civil War.

(Reliable score for task-based, poorly designed, success criteria "The Civil War That Tore? Battles More Than Four": Claim = 4, Historical References = 4, Length = 4, Supporting Details = 4, Persuasion = 1, Creative Title = 4; Total Score = 21/24)

"The Gettysburg Address" by Abraham Lincoln

"Fourscore and seven years ago our fathers brought forth, on this continent, a new nation, conceived in liberty, and dedicated to the proposition that all men are created equal. Now we are engaged in a great civil war, testing whether that nation, or any nation so conceived, and so dedicated, can long endure. We are met on a great battle-field of that war. We have come to dedicate a portion of that field, as a final resting-place for those who here gave their lives, that that nation might live. It is altogether fitting and proper that we should do this. But, in a larger sense, we cannot dedicate, we cannot consecrate—we cannot hallow—this ground. The brave men, living and dead, who struggled here, have consecrated it far above our poor power to add or detract. The world will little note, nor long remember what we say here, but it can never forget what they did here. It is for us the living, rather, to be dedicated here to the unfinished work which they who fought here have thus far so nobly advanced. It is rather for us to be here dedicated to the great task remaining before us—that from these honored dead we take increased devotion to that cause for which they here gave the last full measure of devotion—that we here highly resolve that these dead shall not have died in vain—that this nation, under God, shall have a new birth of freedom, and that government of the people, by the people, for the people, shall not perish from the earth."

(Reliable score for task-based, poorly designed, success criteria "The Gettysburg Address": Claim = 2, Historical References = 1, Length = 2, Supporting Details = 0, Persuasion = 4, Creative Title = 0; Total Score = 9/24)

It is painfully clear that the second essay is of much better quality than the first, so why did it score so poorly? Based on the success criteria, both

Figure 6.1

Non-Exemplar: Task-Based, Nontransferable Success Criteria

Task and Prompt: *In a written paragraph, state and support a claim about an important battle, or battles, during the Civil War. Use the success criteria to develop your response.*

	1	2	3	4
Claim	No claim stated	Claim can't be proven	Claim is an opinion	Claim is first sentence and supported with facts throughout the essay
Historical References	Mentions one battle	Mentions two battles	Mentions three battles	Mentions four or more battles
Length	8 sentences or less	9–10 sentences	11–12 sentences	13 or more sentences
Supporting Details	One detail in support of first sentence	Two details in support of first sentence	Three details in support of first sentence	Four or more details in support of first sentence
Persuasion	Not persuasive	Somewhat persuasive	Persuasive	Very persuasive
Creative Title	Title is not creative	Title is sort of creative	Title is creative	Title is very creative

essays were scored accurately and reliably. However, the success criteria resulted in an invalid inference because they fail to articulate important, transferable attributes of high-quality writing. The arbitrary success criteria don't only result in a system of invalid and unreliable scores and grades, they mislead students to focus on random clutter that is *easy* to measure rather than clarifying what is *important* to measure.

Now, consider the same prompt and writing samples as aligned to a valid, reliable scale for success criteria for *Ideas and Analysis in Writing* from the College Board as shown in Figure 6.2. Read the success criteria, noting the most important differences in important attributes of quality as described at each level. Reread the writing samples to see how they align to these success criteria. The qualitative descriptors are challenging to score, but with a bit of training, they can be used to accurately describe the relationship between the quality of the most important evidence as aligned to the most relevant, transferrable, attributes of quality.

Figure 6.2

Exemplar: Transferable, Prioritized Success Criteria

Task and Prompt: *In a written paragraph, state and support a claim about an important battle, or battles, during the Civil War. Use the success criteria to develop your response.*

Developing (1)	Adequate (2)	Well-developed (3)	Effective (4)
The writer fails to generate an argument that responds intelligibly to the task. The writer's intentions are difficult to discern. Attempts at analysis are unclear or irrelevant.	The writer generates an argument that responds to multiple perspectives on the given issue. The argument's thesis reflects some clarity in thought and purpose. The argument establishes a limited or tangential context for analysis of the issue and its perspectives. Analysis is simplistic or somewhat unclear.	The writer generates an argument that productively engages with multiple perspectives on the given issue. The argument's thesis reflects precision in thought and purpose. The argument establishes and employs a thoughtful context for analysis of the issue and its perspectives. The analysis addresses implications, complexities and tensions, and/or underlying values and assumptions.	The writer generates an argument that critically engages with multiple perspectives on the given issue. The argument's thesis reflects nuance and precision in thought and purpose. The argument establishes and employs an insightful context for analysis of the issue and its perspectives. The analysis examines implications, complexities and tensions, and/or underlying values and assumptions.

For purposes of this example, Levels 1, 3, 5, and 6 from the original rubric (*Ideas and Analysis* from the College Board's ACT Writing Rubric) are presented as 1, 2, 3, and 4.

Once we rate the essays against these valid success criteria, the writing samples can be judged accurately and produce valid, reliable scores. By emphasizing transferable, timeless attributes of high-quality writing, such as *multiple perspectives, nuanced thesis,* and providing *insightful context,* the descriptors in the College Board success criteria read like a running narrative of the most important characteristics of high-quality writing that Lincoln likely had in mind as he penned "The Gettysburg Address." On this valid, reliable scale, Lincoln's writing can accurately and reliably be described as

"Highly Effective" because it demonstrates evidence of the important, relevant criteria articulated at level 4. On the other hand, once the task-driven criteria from the poorly designed, invalid success criteria in the first example are removed, "The Civil War That Tore? Battles More Than Four" is revealed to be a poorly written essay that has no discernable elements of quality that can be transferred to any other writing task. The student has strung together a series of unistructural facts but has not demonstrated deeper understanding. On the valid scale, this essay can accurately and reliably be described as "Developing" because it demonstrates evidence of the relevant criteria articulated at level 1.

Only if both the assessment task and the success criteria are based on important, relevant evidence can we make an accurate, valid inference about the quality of students' evidence and the depth of their understanding as related to standards. Misalignment can lull students into a false sense of accomplishment if their work is inaccurately deemed to be of high quality. Likewise, if their work is deemed to be of low quality—but the assessment process was invalid—students may mistakenly attribute their poor performance to low ability and come to believe they don't have the capacity to produce high-quality work. If this happens repeatedly, they will eventually stop trying.

Reliable Inferences: Action Steps

Reliable inferences about the quality of student work and about each student's depth of understanding minimizes clutter and creates clarity for teaching and learning. To make reliable inferences from assessment evidence, use the following action steps:

- Describe the quality of assessment evidence in terms of relevant success criteria.
- Describe the depth of student understanding while accounting for the context of the assessment task.
- Gather metacognitive evidence to make thinking skills observable.
- Establish interrater reliability among teachers.

Action Step 1

Describe the quality of assessment evidence in terms of relevant success criteria. We've already put important elements in place to ensure we can make reliable inferences about the quality of students' work and their depth of understanding. First, we established priority standards and aligned them to a scale for shared success criteria to focus our collective efforts on what is most important to understand and what it means to understand. Next, we used those standards and scales to intentionally design assessment tasks to gather important evidence of understanding as aligned to different levels of success criteria. Now we can use the evidence and scales to describe the quality of the assessment evidence as related to the most relevant level of the success criteria. To ensure our descriptions of student work are based on reliable inferences, it's not enough to simply know if a response is right or wrong. We also need to acknowledge the limits of what can, and can't, be inferred from specific assessment evidence.

For an example of what this process looks like in the classroom, let's consider the intentionally designed prompt at the unistructural level from the previous chapter: "Which of the following is an example of a sedimentary rock?" Suppose a student correctly answers *sandstone*. The response to the prompt is correct, but what does that mean relative to the success criteria? To answer this question, we need to acknowledge the limits of the inference warranted from the evidence. This item has been designed to gather evidence of knowledge of an academic term at the unistructural level. Therefore, you are limited to making an inference at that level. The inference that "this student understands how sedimentary rocks are formed" is not warranted. To make an inference at that level, the student would have to produce evidence from a more complex task that required him or her to describe and explain that geological process at the relational level.

Figure 6.3 shows how reliable inferences can be made from valid assessment evidence as aligned to different levels of success criteria. It's important not to confuse the quantity of evidence with the depth of evidence. Evaluating the accuracy of evidence at the unistructural or multistructural level is straightforward; surface-level knowledge is usually right or wrong.

Figure 6.3

Aligning Assessment Evidence to Inferences About Quality of Work and Depth of Understanding

	Unistructural	Multistructural	Relational	Extended Abstract
If general scale for success criteria are:	*Defines terms or follows simple procedures.*	*Describes parts and follows multi-step procedures.*	*Connects, compares, and explains relationships between content and concepts or strategically engages in complex procedures.*	*Transfers skills and understandings to new topics, concepts, or contexts to engage in, and reflect on, one's approach to strategizing and solving authentic, open-ended problems.*
Then aligned tasks are:	• tell • "definition is" • "give and solve" • "see and do" • replicate	• tell more • "definitions/ parts are" • "give and solve more" • "see and do more" • "replicate more"	• Constructed response • Conceptual explanations • Scaffolded components of performance task • Non-routine math with justification • "Predict what would"	• Authentic, complex performance/ problem-solving task • Open ended; requires organizing information and explaining one's rationale • Open-ended, provide specific examples that demonstrate general principles
Therefore, a valid inference (if evidence is of high quality) is:	• accurate • correct • consistent	• accurate • partially accurate • correct • partially correct • consistent	• previous level + • clear • fluent • detailed • strategic • effective	• previous levels + • transfer • sophisticated • insightful • novel • elegant

continued

Figure 6.3 (continued)

Aligning Assessment Evidence to Inferences About Quality of Work and Depth of Understanding

	Unistructural	Multistructural	Relational	Extended Abstract
However, limits of valid inferences include:	• Can't infer beyond unistructural level. • Can infer awareness, but not necessarily knowledge. • Can infer ability to do skill in isolation, but not multiple steps. • Too many resources or supports may invalidate inference.	• Can't infer beyond multistructural level. • Can infer awareness multiple terms/parts; but not understanding. • Can infer ability to do multiple steps, but not in authentic contexts. • Too many resources or supports may invalidate inference.	• Can't infer beyond relational level. • Can infer understanding of relationships among content, concepts, skills, but cannot infer transfer. • Absence of resources or supports may invalidate inference. • Too many resources or supports may invalidate inference.	• If there is prerequisite content that the student doesn't know, that may invalidate inferences about understanding of complex skills. • Absence of resources or supports may invalidate inference. • Too many resources or supports may invalidate inference.
Therefore, a reliable inference about the learner is:	Based on this evidence, I can infer that the student is familiar with definitions of some academic terms and can follow simple procedures.	Based on this evidence, I can infer that the student can describe elements or parts of systems or can combine terms and follow multi-step procedures.	Based on this evidence, I can infer that the student can connect, compare, and explain relationships between content and concepts or strategically engage in complex procedures.	Based on this evidence, I can infer that the student can transfer skills and understandings to new topics, concepts, or contexts to engage in, and reflect on an approach to strategizing and solving authentic, open-ended problems.

However, adding more assessment items at these levels does not allow for an inference of deep understanding.

• For example, if a student answers 3 of 10, or 30 of 100, unistructural items correctly, then the same inference is warranted: "The student made frequent errors in defining basic terms and made frequent mistakes in following or replicating simple procedures."

- Likewise, if a student answers 9 of 10, or 90 of 100, unistructural items correctly, then the same inference is warranted: "The student accurately defined most of the basic terms and accurately followed or replicated simple procedures."

For the student who answered 90 of 100 surface-level knowledge items correctly, the evidence does *not* warrant an inference that the student has demonstrated deep understanding of the concepts and skills in this prioritized standard area. This inference is not warranted because there is no evidence generated at the relational or the extended abstract levels of understanding for this concept or skill.

Action Step 2

Describe the depth of student understanding while accounting for the context of the assessment task. In the previous section, we focused on the importance of making valid, reliable inferences about the quality of assessment evidence as related to success criteria. Now we turn our attention to making valid, reliable inferences about students' depth of understanding by acknowledging the relationship between the assessment evidence and the assessment process.

A useful example for understanding the importance of context as related to an assessment task—that most adults remember vividly—is taking your driver's test. For the evaluator to make a valid, reliable inference about your ability as a driver, many different elements had to be aligned:

- The success criteria had to focus on the most important standards for knowing the rules of the road and fluently completing a variety of important driving tasks.
- The driving test needed to be designed to intentionally elicit evidence aligned to the most important success criteria.
- The vehicle couldn't obscure your ability or provide too much assistance.

- The conditions couldn't obscure your ability or provide too much assistance.

We've already discussed the importance of the first two points to ensure the success criteria were prioritized and focused and the task was intentionally designed to gather valid evidence. Now let's look at the next two points related to the context of the assessment. Understanding the context clarifies how resources and conditions can influence the quality of the evidence in a manner that can distort an evaluator's ability to make accurate inferences—in this case, about the driver's skills and understandings. Consider how the context of the driver's test could distort the evaluator's ability to make accurate inferences about two different student drivers.

Student 1 excelled in her driver's education classes and is, legitimately, an *A+* or *advanced* driver. Consider how the context of her driver's test described in the scenarios that follow will distort her evaluator's ability to make accurate inferences about her knowledge and skills:

- She takes her test in a car that has erratic brakes and a broken steering column. Even under ideal driving conditions, she approaches every turn and each intersection with caution. Not knowing if the brakes or steering will be overly sensitive or nearly useless, she stops too early or far too late at every intersection.
- She takes her test on a busy road in a foreign country with dozens of unfamiliar flashing signals and street signs written in a language she doesn't understand. Without being able to discern any meaning, she panics and hits another car.

Student 2 has struggled in his driver's education classes and is, legitimately, a *C–* or *basic* driver. When another car drives past him, he always panics. Consider the effect of the context of his driver's test in the scenarios that follow:

- He shows up to his test in a Tesla self-driving car. Every aspect of his driving is perfect.
- He is scheduled to take his test at 6:00 a.m. on a Saturday morning. There aren't any other cars on the road during his entire test. His performance goes well beyond his wildest expectations.

What inference would the evaluator make about their respective performances? Driver 1 would fail her driver's test in both scenarios despite being a good driver. In the first scenario, the assessment vehicle obscured her ability to demonstrate her skills and understandings. In the second, the assessment conditions obscured her ability to demonstrate her skills and understandings. The evaluator would make an accurate inference from the evidence (*fail*) but an inaccurate inference about her actual skills and understandings.

Driver 2 would pass his driver's test despite being a mediocre driver. In the first scenario, the assessment vehicle provided too much assistance and concealed his inability. In the second, the ideal conditions meant he didn't have to reveal his inability. The evaluator would make an accurate inference from the evidence (*pass*) but an inaccurate inference about his actual skills and understandings.

By considering the context in which assessment evidence is gathered, we can more accurately infer what assessment evidence tells us about a student's depth of understanding. Let's look at the following four examples to better understand how context can invalidate our inferences about students' understanding. Assume for each task that the student gives the correct answer if the item requires surface-level knowledge and a high-quality answer if the response requires deep understanding.

- Example 1: A student is given three equations and asked which represents Einstein's theory of general relativity:

    1. $y = mx+b$ 2. $e = mc^2$ 3. $v = m/d$

- Example 2: As you walk down the hallway of your middle school, you notice a science teacher has hung up student posters describing the process of photosynthesis. As you get about halfway past the display, you realize each of the posters—the flower, sunshine, arrows, labels, definitions, and colors—are almost exactly the same.

- Example 3: Students are given a complex word problem in mathematics on a summative assessment task designed to gather evidence of deep understanding. The semantics of the problem are identical to one that students have done a dozen times.

- Example 4: Students are asked to develop and support a claim related to Amelia Earhart's influence on women's rights in the first half of the 20th century. Students are given an article to use as a source, which argues that Earhart was the most influential American woman of the 20th century.

In the first example, the student accurately identifies the unistructural response ($e = mc^2$) correctly. The warranted inferences from this single, multiple-choice item could include that the student made a lucky guess, the student is familiar with the answer (it's the one he knows has something to do with Einstein), or the student knows this as fact. On a multiple-choice item, the student is given a resource (the correct answer is right there) in a context (the incorrect answers could either be absurd or legitimate distractors). More choices and better distractors increase the likelihood that we are making an accurate inference about the student's level of knowledge on a topic, but the *additional* knowledge doesn't allow for an inference of greater *depth* of knowledge. If it's important to assess if students have internalized specific terms or academic content, use short, open responses, fill-in-the-blank items, or well-designed multiple-choice prompts. However, it's important to acknowledge that these items provide a valid inference of awareness or surface-level knowledge—but not deep understanding.

In the second example, the students have accurately modeled and described the components and process of photosynthesis. This appears as though it should warrant an inference of understanding at the multistructural or even relational level. However, given the uniformity of students' posters, it appears as though the students simply redrew the same model from a resource they were given. Although re-creating a model is a good way to get students to slow down and think about a systems-level process and its parts, the inference warranted is that students can do a one-to-one correspondence of objects from one page to another. This is an important skill for students in primary grades, but it has nothing to do with middle school science standards. Don't fool yourself with powerful phrases such as "create a diagram that explains" if what students are actually doing is "re-creating a diagram." If you want to give students time to replicate a model or a framework, you need to acknowledge the limits of the inferences you can make given the context of the task. Follow-up tasks and prompts would be required to warrant an inference of a deeper level of understanding.

In the third example, the word problem on this math assessment appears to give students an opportunity to demonstrate understanding at the relational level. However, if the problem is identical to one they've seen dozens of times, then students may answer the item correctly by plugging in numbers from the sentence frame and applying it to a rote formula they've memorized. A correct response only warrants an inference of understanding at the multistructural level since they've applied multiple steps to a rote algorithm. To warrant an inference of deeper understanding, you'd need to ask students to explain or justify their thinking and reasoning, or modify the sentence frame and see if students can explain how that change requires them to approach the problem in a different way.

In the fourth example, the prompt asks students to develop and support a claim using evidence to demonstrate understanding at the extended abstract level about Amelia Earhart. However, if students are given a resource that has already accomplished the task for them, we have to account for how that distorts the evidence. An inference at the extended abstract level is not warranted. If the prompt stated, "Identify the claim, one of the supporting arguments, and the aligned evidence in this essay," then perhaps an inference would be warranted at the multistructural level. As with the second example, if you think you are gathering evidence at the extended abstract level—yet students' responses are all remarkably similar—then the context of the task has probably invalidated your inferences of deep understanding.

Making accurate inferences about student understanding based on assessment evidence is an important, yet deceptively challenging, component of teaching. Not only do we need to align prompts, tasks, standards, evidence, and success criteria to ensure assessments are valid and reliable, we also need to consider the context of the assessment task. The resources and conditions given or denied during the assessment process can distort our ability to make accurate, reliable inferences about students' level and depth of understanding and confound our ability to support their strategic efforts to learn.

Action Step 3

Gather metacognitive evidence to make thinking skills observable. Sometimes skills appear in standards and success criteria that aren't necessarily observable by gathering traditional, content-driven assessment evidence. These types of standards typically require students to make decisions and apply strategic effort to attain a specific outcome. For example, students may be asked to "persevere to solve complex problems through the use of a variety of strategies" in mathematics or "develop, revise, and then justify the use of a model" in science. The challenge in assessing these types of evidence is that we can't necessarily infer a student's strategic intent based solely on his or her completion of the academic task.

For example, if a student completes a complex math problem, I don't necessarily have evidence that he or she "persevered" or "tried a variety of strategies." Perhaps the student already knew how to solve the problem efficiently. Conversely, a student may be confronted by a type of math problem he or she has never seen before, attempt a few different solutions, realize the answer isn't reasonable, and then deconstruct the problem and attempt an insightful novel approach—but run out of time and not even answer the question. This student clearly engaged in the important thinking skills described in the standard but did not have a chance to provide evidence of the articulated skills. To gather evidence related to these ways of thinking, we need to ask specific questions that make students' internal thinking visible. This internal voice that guides, or inhibits, one's strategic efforts to learn is called metacognition (Flavell, 1979).

Metacognition can be translated from Greek to mean "thinking about one's own thinking." Teachers can gather evidence about students' metacognition by asking them to write or verbalize their thought processes when planning, monitoring, and evaluating their own learning (Cambridge International Teaching and Learning Team, 2019). Even more powerfully, when students are taught to develop and listen to a productive, strategic metacognitive voice, they are empowered to think more clearly about the relationships among their goals, strategy, and effort. David Perkins (1992) describes four levels of metacognition. By understanding these four levels, we can make better inferences about how students' alignment of goals, strategy, and effort reveals their depth of understanding:

1. *Tacit* learners are unaware of the links among goal, strategy, and effort. They look at a task and determine they either simply "know" the answer or are incapable.
2. *Aware* learners have a sense of the steps required to solve a problem, but they don't strategize by planning, monitoring, or evaluating their progress. Their attempts are mechanistic.
3. *Strategic* learners looks for patterns and relationships among the goal, their effort, and their strategy. They have a sense of what quality looks like, break the problem into smaller parts, plan a strategy, and engage in the necessary work.
4. *Reflective* learners do what strategic learners do but also monitor the effectiveness of their strategies in real time and evaluate the effectiveness of their approach. They revise and modify their strategies based on the relationship between their evidence and the success criteria.

As Figure 6.4 shows, if we only asked for an answer but not an explanation, we would infer that the first student didn't know the answer and the other three students understood equally. By asking the second, metacognitive prompt, students reveal their depth of understanding as related to how they strategize and prioritize their efforts to achieve a goal. Furthermore, the four levels of metacognition can be aligned to the SOLO framework.

- The *tacit* approach sees a single, *unistructural* prompt; either you've memorized this as a math fact, or it can't be solved.
- The *aware* approach sees the problem as a series of *unistructural,* rote tasks to be solved separately and then combined as *multistructural* knowledge.
- The *strategic* approach sees the prompt and task at a *relational* level to discern patterns and calculate more efficiently.
- The *reflective* approach seeks the most important patterns between the task and prompt at an *extended abstract* level to generate a different problem that is much easier to solve.

When we see prioritized standards and success criteria that include phrases such as "persevere to solve complex problems" or "develop, revise, and then justify," it should serve as a cue to ask students to explain the *how* or *why* behind their approach. By asking students to respond to prompts that invite metacognition and make their thinking visible, we improve the reliability of our inferences about their depth of understanding. We will talk more about how to develop students' metacognitive voice later in this book when we discuss ways to support productive responses to opportunities to learn.

Figure 6.4

Examples of Four Types of Metacognition

The Problem	How a Metacognitive Task Reveals Depth of Understanding
Academic prompt: Solve the problem. Show your work. 19 $\times$ 8 = *Metacognitive task:* Using your mathematics vocabulary, write each step of what you did to explain exactly how you got your answer.	*Student 1 (Tacit):* I'm not sure what 19 $\times$ 8 is, so I couldn't do it.
	Student 2 (Aware): I multiplied 9 and 8, and I know that is 72. Then I brought down the 2 and carried the 7 over by the 1. Then I took the 8 and added it to the 7 and got 15. But I would write the 15 next to the 2 because I already brought down the 2. So that would be 152.
	Student 3 (Strategic): I know 9 times 8 is 72. I know 8 times 10 is 80. I added 80 to 72. I got a 2 in the ones column, a 5 in the tens column, and a 1 in the hundreds column. So it's 152.
	Student 4 (Reflective): I looked at the problem and realized the most efficient approach is to think of it as 20 groups of 8, which equals 160. Take away one group of 8, and the answer is 152.

Action Step 4

Establish interrater reliability among teachers. How can expectations such as *analyze, synthesize, evaluate,* or *describe* be assessed reliably when they are so subjective? As Virginia Apgar's assessment of infant health has shown, assessing something complex with a high degree of reliability is absolutely possible. All that is required is a bit of calibration around publicly accessible success criteria that have been aligned to the most important observable evidence.

Consider two simple assessment scenarios. The first has two people debating which type of ice cream is best. One person argues for chocolate, and the other argues for vanilla. After their debate, they agree to disagree which is best and instead agree that one's preference for ice cream is merely subjective. Our inferences about the quality of evidence are always subjective and unreliable when they are based on personally defined success criteria.

However, what if these two individuals were asked to objectively align how different types of ice cream meet specific, clearly defined success criteria for sweetness, richness, and consistency of texture? What if they were also given the opportunity to calibrate their discerning tastebuds by sampling types of ice cream that a panel of experts had categorized, in rank order, based on those attributes? Once the success criteria are shared and calibrated to specific examples, anything can be objectively evaluated in a manner that is accurate and reliable.

Interrater reliability describes the extent that different evaluators rate similar work samples in similar ways. To establish interrater reliability, we need to collaborate and calibrate our shared understanding of what success criteria mean as related to specific examples of student work. With a bit of practice, any teacher within a particular grade should be able to look at evidence of learning from an intentionally designed and aligned assessment item and score that evidence reliably as related to shared success criteria.

How to establish interrater reliability among a team of teachers:

1. Design and administer a valid assessment task that elicits observable evidence of the prioritized standard at a specific level of rigor articulated in the shared success criteria.

2. Establish anchors. Select three work samples representative of evidence for low, moderate, and high-quality work as related to the success criteria (for a total of nine samples). A small group of raters establishes anchors by reviewing and individually scoring the nine work samples. The group then works to establish consensus around an accurate score for each work sample by aligning and describing the most important evidence to the most relevant success criteria. The process must be rooted in evidence and inference rather than opinions. Useful language

includes "I see the student has written. . . . This aligns to the rubric descriptor that reads . . ." If a level of success criteria does not accurately describe evidence in a work sample, then a work sample that shows evidence of that criteria needs to be found or created.

3. Annotate and publish work samples for teachers and students to use as anchors. Annotate how the samples exemplify the success criteria with descriptive statements that connect the specific evidence to specific attributes of the success criteria:

> This sample was scored as a 3 for "Uses Sources as the Basis for Evidence." The underlined phrases are examples of evidence where it effectively uses "a well-selected quote to justify the evidence statement," and a "general rationale for why that specific statement was selected" as described at level 3. It doesn't provide "a detailed rationale for why that specific statement was better than another piece of evidence," as required at level 4.

4. Use published work samples to calibrate a shared understanding of how evidence aligns to success criteria. Once anchors have been established, use the annotated work samples in professional development or collaborative sessions among teachers to calibrate how to assess evidence accurately and reliably. The annotated work samples should also be used in formative lessons with students to help clarify the relationship between success criteria and assessment evidence.

By establishing interrater reliability among teachers, we ensure that our inferences about the quality of students' work and their depth of understanding are consistent and accurate. By aligning these expectations, we can consistently and clearly describe how the most important assessment information aligns to the most relevant success criteria across lessons, units, and courses to more efficiently help our students prioritize their strategic efforts to learn. For a summary of instructional practices to discard to avoid clutter, collective efforts to embrace to minimize the clarity paradox, and action steps to choose clarity to ensure reliable inferences about student learning, see Figure 6.5.

Reliable Inferences: Revisiting the Scenarios

In the first scenario (She gets high scores in the class; low scores on the exam), the rigor of the course and the actual assessment are not aligned. The misalignment between the teacher's expectations and the rigor of the external assessment lulled the student into a false sense of preparedness. Due to this misalignment, the student's inference that she was prepared to do well on the external assessment was invalid.

In the second scenario (Is it explanation or memorization?), the physics question is loaded with verbs that appear to make students' responses to the item worthy of an inference of deep understanding. However, the similarity of the constructed-response answers given by all the students reveal the fact that they've merely memorized an answer and are "knowledge telling." Despite the extended abstract success criteria, the inference warranted from the item is only at the multistructural level.

In the third scenario (We agree what quality looks like), the teachers have established a high level of interrater reliability. They are able to make consistent, accurate inferences about student learning based on the relationship between assessment evidence and success criteria.

Reliable Inferences: Questions for Discussion and Reflection

- How do we ensure consistent, accurate inferences about the quality of evidence from student work?
- How do we ensure consistent, accurate inferences about the depth of student understanding based on valid evidence from student work?
- How do we ensure interrater reliability so we assess evidence of learning as related to shared success criteria in similar ways?
- If components described in this chapter were implemented in our school/district, how might teachers and students benefit after a few years of consistent effort to use them to prioritize students' strategic efforts to learn?

Figure 6.5

Reliable Inferences: Avoiding Clutter, Minimizing the Clarity Paradox, and Choosing Clarity

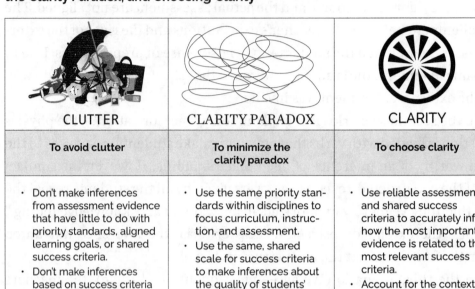

CLUTTER	CLARITY PARADOX	CLARITY
To avoid clutter	**To minimize the clarity paradox**	**To choose clarity**
• Don't make inferences from assessment evidence that have little to do with priority standards, aligned learning goals, or shared success criteria. • Don't make inferences based on success criteria that focus on arbitrary elements of the task. • Don't make inferences about work being of high quality because the student merely follows directions. • Don't assume lower-quality work is due to students' lack of effort.	• Use the same priority standards within disciplines to focus curriculum, instruction, and assessment. • Use the same, shared scale for success criteria to make inferences about the quality of students' work and their depth of understanding. • Use common anchors to exemplify how evidence relates to different levels of success criteria. • Collaborate to calibrate how you assess and score students' work.	• Use reliable assessments and shared success criteria to accurately infer how the most important evidence is related to the most relevant success criteria. • Account for the context of the task when using assessment evidence to make accurate inferences about each student's depth of understanding. • Gather metacognitive evidence to make thinking skills observable. • Establish interrater reliability among teachers.

7

Meaningful Feedback

How can we give feedback that is meaningful to students so they use it to clarify, prioritize, and strategize their next efforts to learn? Consider the following scenarios.

Non-exemplar: I get praise, advice, and grades. Several worksheets from the previous week's activities are returned to a class. José looks through his papers and sees the following:

- 3.5 Good stuff!
- 3 (Not sure what you did on number 7)
- 3
- 2.5 – See comments

He looks at the assignment that scored a 2.5 and sees five or six comments, such as "Nice!" to "We went over this in class (?)" The teacher tells the class that, overall, they did a "good job" but should "be sure to take their time with their work." The teacher then tells them to put their papers in their folders and starts a new lesson.

Exemplar: I get developmental feedback and expectations for revision. A student writes a short paper and completes a self-assessment based on two categories of the school's shared success criteria for writing. The paper is turned in with the self-assessment attached. The student and teacher both score the paper a 3 (out of 4 points) for *Development of Ideas* and 4 (out of 4) for *Organization*. The teacher underlines the elements of the descriptors that justified the 3 rating and circles the elements of the 4 rating that would need to be met to improve. The teacher then writes, "Reread the exemplar essay and underline the verbs and specific details, then reread your essay and do the same. In class tomorrow we'll discuss how you think this could be revised to meet the criteria for a 4."

Exemplar: Opportunities for error identification and self-assessment. A student makes the same error on 8 of 12 math problems. The teacher circles the incorrect problems and writes two simpler problems that isolate the specific step where the student made the errors. She then writes, "Please look at the third step in the items that are wrong on this page. The two problems I've written isolate this step for you. During work time today, come show me how to solve these two problems." The student is able to successfully complete the two problems. In response, the teacher points to the error on the initial assignment and asks, "Do you see what you did here?" When the student indicates that he does, the teacher writes, "In a sentence, state the error you made on these eight problems. In another sentence, state the correct approach. Then re-solve two problems of your choice and bring this back tomorrow so I can revise your score."

Meaningful Feedback

Feedback is information for the learner that clarifies the relationship between their evidence of learning and the most important success criteria. Feedback is meaningful to learners when they can use it to inform or affirm their next efforts to improve. More specifically, feedback is meaningful to learners when 1) it clarifies how their current evidence of learning relates to success criteria, 2) it informs their efforts to prioritize the use of specific strategies to improve, and 3) they use it to take action to improve.

Giving high-quality feedback is an essential aspect of high-quality teaching (Hattie & Timperley, 2007), yet giving feedback is deceptively challenging (Brookhart, 2017). Consider the number of decisions that have to be made when giving feedback. First, the feedback needs to be based on accurate, valid inferences drawn from focused success criteria, intentionally designed tasks, and a reliable evaluator. Given alignment of those elements, teachers need to decide what the feedback should describe, when it should be given, how much should be given, how it can be articulated in a manner that is understood by the learner, and how it should be used by the learner. Give too much feedback too early in the learning process and students may become overwhelmed or too dependent on teachers to rescue them from the hard work of meaning-making (Hattie, 2012). Conversely, wait too long to give feedback and students may internalize errors that are more difficult to correct later (Marzano, 2007).

Given the amount of advice and research available about how teachers can *give* effective feedback, there is surprisingly little discussion of how students can *receive* feedback effectively. This is problematic. As Dylan Wiliam (2016) reminds us, "The only important thing about feedback is what students do with it" (p. 10). Too often, we assume our feedback is seen as useful to learners who will know just what to do with it. However, as Douglas Stone and Sheila Heen (2014) argue in their research on how people receive feedback, this is rarely the case. In fact, they argue that "the ability to receive feedback well is not an inborn trait, but a skill that can be cultivated" (p. 8). To those ends, the true power of feedback is dependent on the extent that the learner perceives it is as meaningful and uses it in productive ways to take action to improve.

Cultivating students' ability to receive feedback in meaningful ways requires us to first empathize with students about why receiving feedback can be difficult. It is easy for us to embrace feedback that praises our sense of self-worth or affirms the quality of our work. But if that is the only feedback we receive, we can find ourselves dependent on praise or mired in a culture of low expectations. It is much harder to receive feedback that is critical of the quality of our work. Rather than acknowledge that there is room to improve, we may become defensive, ignore the feedback entirely, or dismiss the source of the feedback as irrelevant or unfair. Even worse, sometimes when we receive feedback that is critical of the quality of our work, we may begin to engage in internal doubt about our abilities and self-worth. Given our own responses to feedback, we shouldn't be surprised that students—who possess less maturity and more self-doubt—resist feedback or simply ignore it entirely.

If the most important thing about feedback is *what students do with it,* then we need to be intentional about creating conditions in our classrooms where students are open to receiving feedback. These conditions are largely related to students' beliefs about the purpose of schooling and their beliefs about their capacity to be responsive to opportunities to learn. Establishing these conditions is so important, they are the focus of the next two chapters. We'll touch on some of these conditions in this chapter, but our primary focus in this chapter will be on designing feedback that students perceive as meaningful information they can use to prioritize their efforts to learn.

To give feedback that is used by students in meaningful ways requires clarity around three important questions:

- What is the purpose of the feedback?
- What should the feedback describe?
- How can we ensure the meaning of the feedback is clear to the learner?

What is the purpose of the feedback? There are two purposes for feedback: to describe the evidence or to advise the learner. Feedback that is used to *describe* how evidence is related to success criteria is called judgmental feedback. Feedback that is used to *advise* the learner in a manner that affirms or informs a strategy to improve is called developmental feedback.

Judgmental feedback is about evidence and success criteria. This feedback is used to clarify, for the learner, how the most important attributes of the assessment evidence are related to success criteria. High-quality judgmental feedback answers, "What is the quality of the most important evidence as related to the most important success criteria?" For judgmental feedback to be meaningful, it needs to clearly describe the relationship between the evidence and the success criteria in a manner that is timely and understood by the learner.

Developmental feedback is about strategy and forward action. This feedback builds on elements of judgmental feedback about evidence and directs the learner's attention to affirm strategic action. High-quality developmental feedback answers, "Based on the quality of the evidence as related to the success criteria, what should the learner continue to do, or do differently, to improve?" *For developmental feedback to be meaningful, the learner needs to do something with it.* Giving effective developmental feedback is a bit like sending an invitation to a formal event with an RSVP card and a return envelope. We don't simply want to know that the invitation has been sent; we want to make it clear to the recipient that a reply is essential.

What should the feedback describe? When we give feedback to a student, we have to decide what it should describe. Typically, feedback describes one of four areas: compliance, how evidence relates to success criteria, the effectiveness of strategies to attain results, and the learner's sense of self (see Figure 7.1). Compliance with rules or directions includes feedback about logistics of a task, such as "You didn't do Step 3." A description of the quality of the evidence as related to the success criteria includes feedback such as "You've clearly summarized the elements of the story by identifying and describing important details." Feedback that focuses on the effectiveness of the use of strategies directs the learner's attention to where he or she applied effort to achieve results, such as "I can see how you used the two-column chart to put your ideas into distinct categories." Finally, feedback that is focused on the individual's feelings or sense of worth includes statements such as "You did a good job!" or "You should be proud!" Some researchers describe this final type as praise, rather than feedback, because it is focused on the learner's sense of self rather than the relationships among evidence, strategy, and success criteria (Hattie, 2012).

When choosing among the four areas of focus, be aware that feedback about compliance with directions or praise about the learner are least likely to give transferable, actionable information that helps the learner improve. In fact, too much emphasis on these areas creates clutter that can distract students and actually undermine learning (Dweck, 2007; Hyland & Hyland, 2001). For example, if we inundate students with feedback about how well they did or didn't follow specific directions—but fail to focus their attention on important, transferable elements of quality or strategy—then we can mistakenly communicate a message that learning is merely about compliance. Similarly, if we inundate students with praise, we can mistakenly

Figure 7.1

Four Areas of Focus: What Should the Feedback Describe?

Area of Focus	Conditions for Meaningful Feedback	Teacher Designs Effective Feedback to . . .	The Learner Uses the Feedback to . . .
Feedback about compliance with rules or directions	• Clear rules or directions. • Students have necessary skills to follow the rules or directions.	• Determine if the learner correctly followed directions or completed arbitrary steps.	• Clarify expected behaviors. • Follow directions more closely in the future.
Feedback about the quality of evidence as aligned to standards	• Priority standards and shared success criteria are clearly articulated in advance. • Item/task is intentionally designed to align to a specific level of shared success criteria. • Instruction and learning goals are aligned to standards and shared success criteria. • Shared language of assessment. • Student self-assessment.	• Clarify the accuracy of surface-level knowledge or rote steps in a process. • Clarify the quality of a performance or depth of understanding as related to a complex task by identifying or describing the most important and relevant parts. • Help students self-assess and clarify how their perceptions of their work (weaknesses or strengths) align to success criteria.	• Understand content, concepts, and skills. • Identify and correct errors. • Ask clarifying questions. • Revise and clarify work. • Ask important questions that provoke further inquiry. • Prioritize the most important content, concepts, skills that need improvement.
Feedback about the effectiveness of strategies or strategic efforts to improve	• Students see strategy as more important than ability. • Students are asked to self-reflect.	• Clarify the most important relationships between strategy and results. • Help students self-reflect and identify which strategies worked well and which should be refined, revised, or replaced.	• Affirm and inform usefulness of strategies and prioritize strategic efforts to learn. • Ask questions that clarify the strategy. • Refine the use of aligned strategies, as needed, to improve.

| Feedback (as praise) about "me" | • A classroom culture in which students feel safe and supported.
• Teacher and students have a growth mindset. | • Affirm effort.
• Encourage potential and modify strategy to improve.
• Express belief in the capacity of the learner to be effective. | • Support emotional needs/sense of self-worth.
• Feel accepted and valued.
• Persevere through complexity or ambiguity.
• Celebrate success and strategic efforts to improve. |

communicate a message that learning is about feeling good about one's innate ability rather than the effectiveness of one's strategic effort. We'll talk more about how to acknowledge and navigate the complexities of compliance and praise in the upcoming chapters. Given the emphasis of this chapter is on ensuring students use feedback in meaningful ways to improve their learning, we'll focus on feedback that *describes evidence as related to success criteria* and *the effectiveness of strategies to attain results.*

How can we ensure the meaning of the feedback is clear to the learner? To give feedback that is clear to the learner, it should be reliable, objective, and specific. The language and levels of the shared success criteria and shared language of assessment that we discussed in previous chapters provide a common, reliable scale that can be used to make accurate inferences about the quality of students' work and their depth of understanding. Just as we improve the reliability of our inferences by focusing on the most important evidence as related to the most relevant success criteria, reliable feedback communicates information about those elements as well.

To give feedback that is objective, we need to describe the evidence of learning using language of the shared success criteria. To be objective is to describe without bias. When giving objective feedback, the teacher is the conduit that connects the most important evidence to the most relevant descriptors. For example, if the success criteria include descriptors such as "well-chosen details" or "a defensible claim," then the feedback should clarify *how* and *why* the details appear to be well chosen and *how* and *why* the claim was defensible.

Finally, by giving feedback that is specific, we help learners focus on a narrow range of the most important portions of their work as related to the most relevant success criteria. Vague judgmental statements (e.g., those that include words such as *good, poor,* or *nice*) are too arbitrary to be helpful. If learners don't know what elements were *good, poor,* or *nice* and why, they cannot internalize the most important attributes of the evidence that should be transferred, or revised, in the future. Specific feedback draws on the language of the shared success criteria and our shared language of assessment. For example, consider this statement: "Your explanation of the data about your terrarium is clear. You've identified the most relevant elements in the data set, and you've provided direct evidence of how they meet the criteria you've established for an effective solution." Although the feedback is about the academic content related to *terrarium* and *data,* the important elements of the feedback also require the student to understand *explanation, relevance, evidence, criteria,* and what makes a solution effective.

Giving clear feedback that can be used in meaningful ways by students is a highly language-dependent task. There is no way around this. By establishing, articulating, and committing to the constraints of prioritized standards, a shared language of assessment, and focused success criteria, we give students the time, consistency, and clarity necessary to make meaning of the language required of students to receive feedback in meaningful ways to improve their learning. Examples and nonexamples of clear feedback are given in Figure 7.2.

Now that we've established the purpose of feedback (judgment or development), what the feedback should describe (emphasis on evidence of learning as related to success criteria and the effectiveness of one's strategies), and how it can be given in a manner that is clear to students (reliable, objective, specific), we can draw on these elements to design feedback that students use in meaningful ways.

Figure 7.2

Characteristics of Clear Feedback

Component of Quality	Effective Feedback	Ineffective Feedback
Reliable	• Draws on a shared language of assessment, shared success criteria, and a shared, reliable scale for rigor. • Is based on a reliable inference from shared, published success criteria and intentional collection of valid evidence.	• Is based on criteria "in the teacher's head" or hasn't been stated in advance. • Draws on terms and jargon that are not understood by the learner. • Gives a numerical score or grade, but it is unclear what that score or grade means as related to the student's next efforts to learn. • Is compared to other students rather than to the criteria.
Objective	• Objectively describes the evidence as related to the success criteria. • Objectively states, or provokes inquiry about, what the learner should do next.	• Is stated as a subjective opinion with no criteria for quality. • Makes a judgment about effort or behavior rather than evidence of understanding. • Ignores the evidence and gives an invalid rating or score based on preconceived notions of ability.
Specific	• Specifically states the most relevant aspects of the evidence as related to the most important aspects of a specific level of success criteria. • Clarifies specific progress along a shared scale for quality.	• Mistakes precision for specificity. • Simply marked as "right" or "wrong" with no opportunity for student to clarify/understand why. • Is ambiguous or vaguely worded.

Meaningful Feedback: Action Steps

Meaningful feedback minimizes clutter and creates clarity for teaching and learning. To give feedback that students use in meaningful ways to affirm and inform their next efforts to learn, do the following:

- Teach students to use feedback in meaningful ways.
- Give meaningful judgmental feedback.
- Give meaningful developmental feedback.

Action Step 1

Teach students to use feedback in meaningful ways. If we want students to use feedback meaningfully, we must teach them how to receive and use feedback in meaningful ways. Too often, students see the purpose of feedback as purely transactional. A student who has this transactional view may explain feedback along the lines of "I do my work, my teacher gives me a grade, and then we move on to the next thing and repeat the process." Conversely, consider the characteristics of students who use feedback in meaningful ways and the associated "I can" statements in Figure 7.3.

Figure 7.3

Characteristics of Students Who Use Feedback in Meaningful Ways

I use judgmental feedback to clarify how the quality of my work relates to success criteria.	I use developmental feedback to affirm and inform the strategies I use in my next efforts to improve.	I use success criteria and feedback to take action to improve.
• I can explain the success criteria in my own words. • I can describe how my assessment evidence does, or does not, relate to success criteria. • If I don't understand the feedback I am given, I ask clarifying questions.	• I use feedback to affirm what I am doing well. • I use feedback to inform my strategic efforts to improve. • If I don't understand what to do next to improve my learning, I ask clarifying questions.	• I use success criteria to plan my work. • I monitor how my evidence is related to the success criteria to be sure I am using an effective strategy. • I use feedback to affirm my successes and inform my ongoing efforts to improve.

Even though these "I can" statements don't appear in state standards or curriculum guides, they are every bit as important as any other content or skills we teach. Students are more likely to use feedback in meaningful ways when they understand how it can be used to 1) clarify how their evidence of learning relates to success criteria, 2) affirm and inform their use of strategies, and 3) take action to improve. As was discussed at the beginning of this chapter, these skills are not innate. To teach students how to use feedback, consider the following strategies:

- **Teach students how evidence relates to success criteria.** Be clear about how the specific language of your shared success criteria are used to describe high-quality work. For example, if *explanation* and *justification* appear frequently in your priority standards and success criteria, then they should be the focus of vocabulary acquisition lessons, learning goals, assessment tasks, and written feedback.

- **Teach students to identify important distinctions among different levels of success criteria.** Have students identify and underline important differences among different levels of success criteria. For example, say, "Look at the proficient and advanced descriptors for 'Arguments and Claims.' Underline the words that are identical and circle the words that are different. Then we'll discuss . . ."
- **Teach students how success criteria can be used to describe assessment evidence.** Provide students with samples of high-quality assessment evidence (e.g., an anonymous sample from a previous class, the internet, or an example you've made up) and ask students to use the success criteria to describe evidence of quality. Use a sentence frame such as "I see [specific aspect of work] as evidence of [specific aspect of success criteria]." For example, "I see 'from Day 5 to Day 10, the rate of increase more than doubled to 1.2 cm per day' as evidence of 'clearly articulating a pattern in the data.'" This can also be done with non-exemplars; for example, "I see 'the plants got bigger' as evidence of a vague generalization."
- **Teach students how assessment evidence can be sorted by specific attributes.** Give students samples of assessment evidence and ask them to sort the samples into different levels of quality based on specific criteria and justify their rationale using the language of the success criteria.
- **Teach students to use success criteria to self-assess.** Self-assessment occurs when learners describe their own assessment evidence as related to success criteria to make a judgment about the quality of their work. High-quality self-assessment answers the questions *How would I describe the quality of my evidence as related to the success criteria, and what have I learned?* Self-assessment can—and should—happen all the time. When students complete various assignments or assessments, they can turn them in with rubrics or learning goals where they

have judged their own evidence based on success criteria and justified their rating. The more proficient a learner is at accurately assessing his or her own work, the more likely that student is able to prioritize and strategize next efforts to learn. Additionally, students who can self-assess are more responsive to feedback because they understand how feedback works.

- **Teach students to use success criteria to self-reflect.** Self-reflection occurs when learners describe the effectiveness of their strategic efforts to learn. High-quality self-reflection answers the questions *What strategies were effective in my efforts to produce high-quality work, and what have I learned?* The most powerful aspect of self-reflection is that it empowers the learner to transfer understandings and strategies to new problems and contexts. When students complete various assignments or assessments, they can turn them in with a written reflection related to what strategies were useful, which weren't, and how they might use their understanding of strategies and results to prioritize their time or effort in the future.

- **Teach students that strategy is more important than ability**. If students believe innate ability determines one's outcomes, regardless of strategy, there is little or no value to be responsive to feedback. This statement explains a lot of students' defensiveness about feedback. Establishing classrooms and programs that emphasize strategy over ability is so important, it is discussed in detail in the next two chapters.

Action Step 2

Give meaningful judgmental feedback. Judgmental feedback is about the relationship between evidence and success criteria. It's critical to articulate clear success criteria to establish expectations for quality. In a system designed to maximize learning, judgmental feedback should draw the learner's attention to the most relevant category and level of quality. Articulating a valid, reliable inference about the quality of the most important evidence draws the learner's attention to the most important attributes of their work. Once the relationship between the success criteria and the evidence has been articulated, the teacher can clarify the most important elements of how the goal was attained—or why there is a gap. If judgmental feedback is to be meaningful, the learner needs to understand what it means. It also needs to be delivered in a manner that is timely, which means it can be used to affirm current efforts or inform next efforts to correct errors and modify misconceptions. Examples of descriptive, judgmental feedback are shown in Figure 7.4.

Here are some helpful strategies to ensure high-quality judgmental feedback:

- **State it clearly.** Use your shared success criteria and shared language of assessment as the basis for clear, descriptive feedback.
- **Give it objectively.** Judgmental feedback is, simply, about the evidence and the success criteria. State the information that is the basis for the inference. "I see . . . This demonstrates evidence of the success criteria because . . ." or "This evidence does not meet the success criteria because . . ."
- **Keep it focused.** Focus on the most important evidence as related to the most important success criteria. Only use relevant portions of success criteria on a given task as the basis for feedback.
- **Align feedback to the level of success criteria.** For tasks designed to demonstrate evidence of surface-level knowledge, students' responses can simply be judged as right or wrong. For more complex tasks designed to demonstrate deep understanding, students' responses require a rubric or qualitative descriptor that describes the important attributes of the response.
- **Make it manageable for students.** If there are significant gaps between the evidence and the success criteria, focus on a portion of the work that is representative of that gap and provide specific, focused feedback rather than documenting every error.
- **Don't bury important concerns behind vague praise.** When we hide important concerns behind vague praise, students may internalize the praise and ignore the concerns. Avoid saying, "You did a good job on many parts of this project! It was very interesting. You didn't use any sources, though, and none of your evidence supports your claims."

Figure 7.4

Examples of High-Quality Judgmental Feedback

	Unistructural	Multistructural	Relational	Extended Abstract
If general scale for success criteria is:	*Defines terms or follows simple procedures.*	*Describes or combines terms and follows multistep procedures.*	*Connects, compares, or explains relationships between content and concepts or strategically engages in complex procedures.*	*Transfers skills and understandings to new topics, concepts, or contexts to engage in, and reflect upon, my approach to strategizing and solving authentic, open-ended problems.*
Then examples of aligned judgmental feedback include:	• + You've accurately defined/used *basic academic language.* • + You've correctly completed *simple procedure.* • - You've incorrectly . . . /made errors or omissions (*see above*).	• + You've accurately defined/used *complex academic language.* • + You've correctly followed *multi-step procedure.* • - You've incorrectly . . . /made errors or omissions on (*see above*).	• + You've given a clear/accurate/coherent explanation, connection, comparison: among *content, or between content and concepts.* • + You've selected an *efficient/effective procedure,* and fluently/accurately applied *complex procedure.* • - You've made errors, omissions, lack of fluency (*see above*).	• + Given *unfamiliar examples or contexts,* you've made relevant connections among *content and concepts* to generate a warranted *solution or response.* • + Given an open-ended problem, you've determined, applied and justified an effective strategy. • - Given an open-ended problem, you've made errors, omissions, lack of fluency in (*see above*).

	Unistructural	Multistructural	Relational	Extended Abstract
Therefore, specific examples of aligned, meaningful judgmental feedback are:	• "You've accurately used the terms *sum* and *product*." • "Yes, you gave each quarternote one full beat." • "You've confused *scene* with *setting*." • "Your measurement of *1.5 inches* is incorrect."	• "You've identified and defined *numerator* and *denominator* accurately." • "Your measurements and calculation of the *surface area* are both accurate." • "You gave an example of mitosis; but you did not state the definition." • "You selected a *relevant quote*, but did not give the *source*."	• "You've *interpreted the graph* and explained the relationship among variables accurately; there is a *linear relationship between variables A and B*." • "You've used coordinates of latitude and longitude to accurately re-construct the map." • "Your explanation of how multiplication is repeated addition is clear and accurate." • "Your explanation of the difference between a linear and quadratic relationship doesn't include the essential attribute of rate of change."	• "Your explanation of how the results would have been different if there was less oxygen in the environment is plausible and supported by your data." • "Your justification of how the story would have ended if Goldilocks hadn't fallen asleep on the bed makes sense given how you've described her character traits." • "Your proposed solution of allocating more resources on the third day in the simulation clearly meets the criteria you've established for an effective solution."

- **Make it manageable for you.** If you find yourself writing or typing feedback that describes the same errors or omissions across many examples of student work, ask yourself if the assessment prompt or the directions need to be clarified. If they are as clear as possible, consider changing the success criteria. If these elements are aligned and you find yourself inundated with more work than you can assess—let alone give high-quality feedback about—consider giving students shorter, more focused prompts and tasks.

- **Give frequent feedback but grade only when you have to.** Grading too early in the learning process can cause students to ignore important, descriptive, judgmental feedback. Teachers aren't required to put a grade on everything, so don't fall into the trap of grading every assignment. Grading is clerical. Feedback improves learning.

Action Step 3

Give meaningful developmental feedback. Although high-quality judgmental feedback clarifies how evidence relates to success criteria, high-quality developmental feedback prioritizes the learner's next efforts to improve. Imagine being lost in an unfamiliar city. Judgmental feedback will help you clarify relevant landmarks to identify your current location; by contrast, developmental feedback will help you determine a route to get to your destination.

Developmental feedback builds on judgmental feedback and draws the learner's attention to what he or she should do next. It is about strategy and action. If the student's assessment evidence is aligned to high-quality indicators at the intended level of success criteria, feedback can be used to affirm current understandings and help the student "scaffold up" toward the next level of quality (see Figure 7.5). If the work does not demonstrate evidence of quality at the intended level of success criteria, the feedback can be used to help the student "step back" to correct errors or omissions or to clarify misunderstandings (see Figure 7.6).

Before we discuss strategies we can use to ensure high-quality developmental feedback, let's discard developmental feedback that merely causes clutter. If you've ever spent an entire weekend grading and writing thoughtful comments and important advice on student papers only to watch students glance at their grades before putting the paper in a folder (or the trash), you've got a feedback-related clutter problem. Students often respond to feedback in this way when 1) there is no expectation that they do anything other than receive it, 2) it is based on assumptions about their effort rather than evidence of strategy, or 3) they are overwhelmed by the amount of advice that has been given.

Figure 7.5
___

Developmental Feedback for Evidence That Meets Aligned Success Criteria

	Unistructural	Multistructural	Relational	Extended Abstract
If success criteria and assessment evidence allow for an inference that:	The student is able to • memorize (in isolation) • identify (isolated parts) • define/give (basic) • recall • follow rote steps	The student is able to • memorize (and apply) • identify (characteristics) • define (complex) • give (complex) • describe • classify • follow rote steps • organize	The student is able to • compare and contrast • explain (known) • given claim/ evidence; argue • given a framework; analyze • apply to similar context • perform fluently	On open-ended, authentic tasks, the student is able to • design and justify/explain • determine and justify • hypothesize and justify/ explain • generate and explain/ support • generate criteria and analyze/ strategize • interpret and perform fluently
Then specific examples of developmental feedback that affirms evidence and informs strategy are:	"You've accurately identified the definition of sum and product. How might you restate these in your own words?"	"You've identified and defined *sum* and *product* accurately in each example. Your attention to this difference shows me you understand that mathematical thinking is about both numbers and language!"	"Your explanation of how multiplication is repeated addition is clear and uses the terms *sum* and *product* accurately. By defining the key terms and giving examples, it was easy for me to follow along."	"The explanation you've given of how you would do this multiplication problem most efficiently if you could only use addition is well-reasoned and clear. Your specific numerical examples and application of key vocabulary in the statement 'the product of 10 × 5 is another way of saying the sum of 10 + 10 + 10 + 10 + 10' is a concise way to explain mathematical concepts to someone."

continued

Figure 7.5 *(continued)*

Developmental Feedback for Evidence That Meets Aligned Success Criteria

	Unistructural	Multistructural	Relational	Extended Abstract
Therefore, to "scaffold up" in quantitative or qualitative phases, you:	**Knowledge/Skill Acquisition** • Affirm particularly important strategies as related to clarifying elements of, or distinctions among, content and concepts. • Affirm specific aspects of observable strategies or skills. • Begin to scaffold for next level of depth and complexity or ask an open-ended question.		**Deepening Understanding** • Affirm particularly important strategies as related to discerning relationships or critical thinking. • Affirm depth of observable strategies or skills. • Scaffold to next level of depth and complexity or ask an open-ended question.	

Figure 7.6

Developmental Feedback for Evidence That Does Not Meet Aligned Success Criteria

	Unistructural	Multistructural	Relational	Extended Abstract
If success criteria and assessment evidence allow for an inference that:	The student exhibits errors in his/her ability to • memorize (in isolation) • identify (isolated parts) • define (basic) • recall • follow rote step • give (basic)	The student exhibits errors in his/her ability to • memorize (and apply) • identify (characteristics) • define (complex) • give (complex) • describe • classify • follow rote steps • organize	The student exhibits errors in his/her ability to • compare and contrast • explain (known) • given claim/ evidence; argue • given framework; analyze • apply to similar context • translate and apply • summarize • interpret meaning • perform fluently	On open-ended, authentic tasks, the student exhibits errors in his/her ability to • design and justify/explain • hypothesize and justify/ explain • generate criteria and analyze • generate criteria and strategize • generate claim and support • evaluate and explain • interpret and perform fluently

	Unistructural	Multistructural	Relational	Extended Abstract
Then, to help students "step back" to a previous level of complexity (so they can correct, revise, or restrategize), you:	• Correct error • Identify error • Guided review/ practice • Apply strategy with guided practice • Try a new strategy	• Clarify prompt, task, or success criteria • Step back and clarify content at a less complex level • Clarify criteria for quality • Ask clarifying questions • Invite self-assessment, self-reflection	• Clarify prompt, task, or success criteria • Step back and clarify basic or complex content or skills at previous level of complexity • Focus attention on a specific aspect of the task • Ask clarifying questions • Invite self-assessment, self-reflection	• Clarify prompt, task, or success criteria • Step back and clarify complex content, concepts, or skills at previous levels of complexity • Ask follow-up questions related to justification of approach as related to success criteria • Ask follow-up questions that challenge student beyond the success criteria • Invite self-assessment, self-reflection
Therefore, specific examples of aligned developmental feedback are:	"You've mistaken sum and product. I've stated the definitions below. Can you restate these in your own words?"	"You've identified the sum and product accurately, but your definition of *sum* is missing an important part. Can you revise your definition to include the word *add*?"	"Your explanation of how multiplication is repeated addition is unclear to me. Using only numbers, +, and ×, show me how you'd write "20 times 5" and "adding 20, 5 times.""	"The explanation you've given of how you would do this multiplication problem most efficiently if you could only use addition is well-reasoned and clear. But you've solved the example incorrectly. Correct your error and show me the right answer."

For example, we often think we are giving actionable feedback when, in fact, we are delivering what David Perkins (2009) describes as ineffective, "hearts and minds" feedback (p. 80). This feedback is typically expressed as something along the lines of "The next time you are asked to write an essay about metamorphic rocks, remember to. . . . Please take this feedback to heart and keep it in mind." Rarely does that specific task come up again, and if it does, students have long forgotten the teacher's advice. Despite the thoughtful intent, the feedback isn't useful because it is rarely taken to heart—nor kept in mind.

Feedback that is based on assumptions about student effort, rather than observable evidence about strategy, also creates clutter. Too often, vague judgmental statements about effort, such as "You need to take your time" or "You need to study more," assumes students know how to do the work, know the success criteria, and know how to prioritize strategies effectively—but simply choose not to. These assumptions confound *will* with *skill* and can inadvertently undermine student effort.

Finally, giving more developmental feedback than students can realistically use to improve simply overwhelms them with clutter. Don't ask students to immediately turn "below basic" evidence into "advanced" evidence; instead, guide them to take meaningful steps to move to the "basic" level.

By discarding developmental feedback that is merely clutter, we help students better understand that the purpose of developmental feedback is to use it to take action to improve. Here are some helpful strategies to ensure students put developmental feedback to use:

- **Expect a response and keep it real.** If you've identified numerous errors, ask students to correct a representative sample of their mistakes. For example, say, "You answered items 1–4 correctly. On items 5–10, you seem to have forgotten about the denominator in the multi-step equation. Correct items 9 and 10, and write the rule for denominators in this type of equation."

- **Give students time to respond.** Build response and revision time into your instructional time. Having students identify and correct errors—or revise their work and state a more accurate conceptualization—is a powerful learning tool.

- **Give students a quick deadline to respond.** When you ask for a specific response to feedback, give students a specific due date. Make it a quick turnaround so the feedback is acted on while it is still relevant to the learner.

- **Keep grades/marks open until you've received a response.** There is nothing that says every piece of work done by every student needs to be graded. Therefore, there's nothing stopping you from saying, "You've defined the terms correctly and given concrete examples, but you haven't compared them as was requested in the prompt. By tomorrow, write a sentence about how X and Y are similar and a sentence about how they are different, and then I'll be able to assess this."

- **Step back to scaffold up.** Step back to identify something specific that students did well, and draw attention to what comes next to meet the success criteria. For example, say, "You clearly know the definitions of the vocabulary in this unit, but the caption you've written for the diagram of how earthquakes occur doesn't include any of that specific vocabulary. Revise your caption using at least four terms from the unit vocabulary list."

- **Affirm the strategy used.** Affirm details that draw students' attention to how their strategies/choices helped them achieve specific components of the learning goal and success criteria. For example, say, "The evidence you selected to support your claim was well chosen. The quote from James Baldwin you selected supports your claim about equal rights and refutes the counterclaim about equal protection."

- **Focus on strategic effort.** Give specific feedback about the quality of the work by affirming what was done well as related to the success criteria. For example, say, "Your summary is effective because it captures the most important ideas in this article in just a few, well-written sentences. What strategy did you use to reach that level of clarity?"

- **Focus on incremental growth.** Give specific feedback when you notice significant progress or particularly effective strategic effort. For example, say, "I remember when we looked at your data tables at the beginning of the year, neither of us could read them. Now you've got the columns and rows clearly labeled and you've left enough space to write your data in each cell. I see you are planning ahead to organize your information so it can be presented clearly."

- **Focus on learning goals, not arbitrary tasks.** Focus on transferable learning goals and not arbitrary tasks. For example, two students create a brochure (task) to explain a process (prompt aligned to success criteria) in an English class. Both students state clear, actionable steps in chronological order using precise, descriptive language. One uses layout and design software; the other writes by hand—clearly but with minimal attention to design. For both students, the feedback should be "You've stated clear, actionable steps in chronological order using precise, descriptive language." Praise the layout whiz, but do not penalize the student who attained the success criteria with less flourish.

- **Scaffold up.** When you see an opportunity for a student to pursue more rigorous content or a more complex skill, scaffold up. For example, say, "Your explanation of how linear equations are different from quadratic equations accurately and clearly addresses the distinctions in rate, slope, and time. Do you know what logarithms are? We'll learn about those in the next unit; you're clearly ready to understand those as well."

High-quality feedback describes how the most important assessment evidence aligns to the most relevant success criteria in a manner that is reliable, objective, and specific. What is most important about feedback is that it is understood and used by students in meaningful ways to clarify, prioritize, and strategize their next efforts to learn. For a summary of indicators of systems-level clarity for meaningful feedback, see Figure 7.7.

Meaningful Feedback: Revisiting the Scenarios

The first scenario (I get praise, advice, and grades) emphasizes points and grades for accountability rather than feedback that can help the learner improve. The feedback isn't specific, timely, or actionable. The written comments that are provided are vague and emphasize effort rather than strategy.

The second scenario (I get developmental feedback and expectations for revision) captures many of the characteristics of meaningful feedback. The shared success criteria and the shared language of assessment allow the teacher to give clear, specific, judgmental feedback to help affirm what the student is doing well—along with developmental feedback to help the student identify what needs to be done to improve. The developmental feedback is given in the form of a specific task that is a strategy to improve (underline the verbs and specific details in the exemplar essay and in your own essay). The student is expected to use this feedback to engage in a self-assessment process that will clarify the most important evidence as related to the most relevant success criteria.

In the third scenario (Opportunities for error identification and self-assessment), the math teacher gives meaningful feedback that helps the student focus on the most important evidence as related to the most important success criteria. In an environment solely focused on grading, the teacher could have simply written 4 of 12 or 33% on the paper. Instead, she notes that the student made the same error eight times. The feedback positions the student to answer each of the following questions: How well does my assessment evidence meet success criteria? What should I do next to prioritize my strategic efforts to improve? How does this help me plan, monitor, and evaluate my work in the future?

Meaningful Feedback: Questions for Discussion and Reflection

- How do I/we give students meaningful judgmental feedback? Developmental feedback?
- How do I/we give feedback that is useful for students to clarify, prioritize, and internalize their efforts to learn?
- How do I/we give students time to engage in meaningful self-assessment and self-reflection?
- If components described in this chapter were implemented in our school/district, how might teachers and students benefit after a few years of consistent efforts to use them to prioritize students' strategic efforts to learn?

Figure 7.7

Meaningful Feedback: Avoiding Clutter, Minimizing the Clarity Paradox, and Choosing Clarity

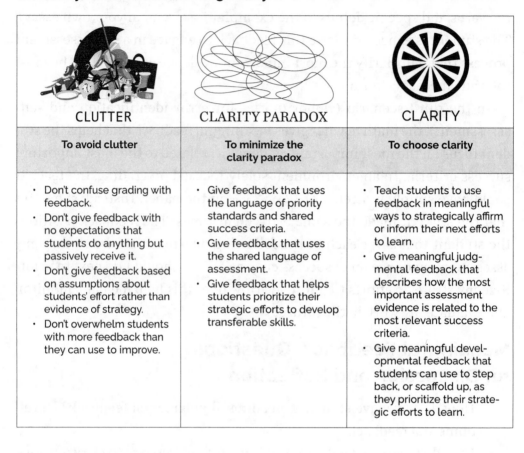

CLUTTER	CLARITY PARADOX	CLARITY
To avoid clutter	**To minimize the clarity paradox**	**To choose clarity**
• Don't confuse grading with feedback. • Don't give feedback with no expectations that students do anything but passively receive it. • Don't give feedback based on assumptions about students' effort rather than evidence of strategy. • Don't overwhelm students with more feedback than they can use to improve.	• Give feedback that uses the language of priority standards and shared success criteria. • Give feedback that uses the shared language of assessment. • Give feedback that helps students prioritize their strategic efforts to develop transferable skills.	• Teach students to use feedback in meaningful ways to strategically affirm or inform their next efforts to learn. • Give meaningful judgmental feedback that describes how the most important assessment evidence is related to the most relevant success criteria. • Give meaningful developmental feedback that students can use to step back, or scaffold up, as they prioritize their strategic efforts to learn.

8

Shared Purpose

How does a shared purpose for teaching and learning minimize clutter and create clarity for teachers and learners? Consider the following scenarios.

Non-exemplar: For Thursday, complete p. 349, 1–23 odds; On Friday, test. A teacher distributes her syllabus on the first day of math class. The syllabus begins with a list of chapters in the textbook that will be covered and a list of the eight mathematical practice standards. The syllabus then describes the materials required for the course: a specific type of binder, calculator, and graph paper. Next, it describes how grades will be determined: 60% summative tests, 20% quizzes (one retake permitted), 15% projects, and 5% formative/homework.

Throughout the year, the teacher writes homework assignments and other important dates on the whiteboard. For example, "Feb 24: p. 345, 1–27 odds; Feb 25: p. 349, 1–21 odds; Mar 3: Unit 12 quiz; Mar 7: Unit 12 test." Each day, the teacher presents and models a computational method, students do a few practice problems, and then they start their homework. The following day, the teacher does a quick visual check to see if students did their homework, shows the correct answers, asks if there are questions, and presents new material. After each unit test, assessments are scored and returned several days later.

The eight mathematics practice standards from the syllabus are rarely discussed or referenced. In fact, a scan of all the assignments students complete throughout the year shows a lot of calculations and formulas but no written responses defining key terms, explaining processes, or justifying solutions.

Exemplar: Developing clarity of purpose; developing deeper understanding. On the first day of math class, the teacher presents a thought-provoking series of sequentially organized symbols and asks students to identify and describe patterns they see. It spurs some thoughtful discussion about order, relationships, and symbols. The teacher then presents a list of essential questions about mathematics. The students are asked to use these questions to make further meaning of the symbols. After several minutes, the class is engaged in a heated discussion about what the "real" pattern is and what it means. At the peak of the debate, the teacher passes out a three-page syllabus.

On the first page of the syllabus, there are the nine essential questions that added fuel to the debate, nine enduring understandings about mathematics, and a list of about 20 key vocabulary terms and concepts for the course. On the second page are a series of nine prioritized standards (the eight math practices and one standard aligned to the specific computations and operations for the course), and a proficiency scale for each. The general scale—which flows from knowing individual/isolated content or skills to justifying solutions to open-ended problems—is familiar to students because it was also used in their math class the previous year. The third page is a brief overview of each unit, including the most important content in each unit and how it aligns to two or three specific categories of the shared success criteria.

In each unit, students do a lot of traditional math problems, but they also frequently write to explain and justify processes, defend claims, and explain mathematical concepts and processes. They use the common proficiency scale and success criteria to monitor their progress toward learning goals. In any given unit, students can tell you what they understand and where they are confused. They come to class with as much work completed as is necessary for them to show—and defend—their claim that they've met the aligned learning goal. If their work is not completed, they come to class with self-assessment statements framed as "What I understand is . . . and where I am getting stuck is . . ."

Students have a unit test every couple weeks. On each test, the problems are specifically and clearly aligned to the unit's learning goals and leveled success criteria. There are a series of questions at the end of each assessment: Was this assessment a fair measure of the learning goals we focused on in this unit? Why or why not? What is something you learned in this unit that is clearer now than when the unit started? What is something I did, or you wish I'd have done, to better support your strategic efforts to learn?

Shared Purpose

In a standards-based system, the purpose of schools is to prioritize each student's strategic efforts to learn clearly articulated standards. That purpose is shared when the system meets three criteria:

- We have a shared understanding of what it means to understand.
- We have a shared understanding of what is most important to understand.
- We prioritize our use of time and strategies to support students' strategic efforts to develop important skills and understandings.

When something is purposeful, it is relevant to a specific goal and strategically useful (Frontier & Mielke, 2016). Planning and articulating a purpose for something only matters if those plans are actively shared and used to guide specific actions. For example, suppose you are working with an architect to design your dream home. It's not enough for you to simply have a vision of what the home should be like. You and the architect need to translate that vision into a plan. Once that plan is established, it needs to be shared with those who will be doing the work—the carpenters, plumbers, and electricians—so they can align their strategic efforts to achieve the shared purpose. Similarly, teachers and learners benefit when they are aware of, and agree on, the purpose of school so they can align their strategic efforts to achieve their shared goals. If those who are doing the work aren't aware of the plan, they cannot align their efforts to intended results.

Fulfilling a shared purpose requires the alignment of beliefs with action. To understand what this looks like in schools, we need to answer three questions:

- What is the purpose of school?
- How do our beliefs about the purpose of school influence our actions?
- How do our actions prioritize students' strategic efforts to succeed?

What is the purpose of school?

Regardless of what it says on the vinyl banner above a school's entrance or what is stated in a school's mission statement, the purpose of a school is determined by the choices and decisions made by the professional educators in that building each day.

The thesis of this book is that in a standards-based system, the purpose of school is to prioritize students' strategic efforts to develop important skills and understandings. To support students' efforts to see through the clutter and focus on what is most important, we have to acknowledge that *what teachers emphasize is what students internalize*. The two scenarios at the beginning of this chapter reveal how teachers' choices can establish dramatically different purposes for learning—even within the same school. The first teacher focused students' effort and attention on compliance related to isolated tasks to cover content, complete assignments, and earn points. Everything was framed in terms of a transaction: you give me your work and I will record the points. The second teacher focused students' effort and attention on learning and emphasized learning, inquiry, success criteria, and meaningful feedback as aligned to standards.

The consistent choices we make in classrooms each day have important consequences for what students perceive to be the purpose of school (see Figure 8.1). By the end of the first quarter in these two classrooms, it would be easy to see how students might ask very different questions of their teachers based on what they believe their teachers value most. If we are going to fulfill our shared purpose to prioritize students' strategic efforts to develop important skills and understandings, we need to create learning-centered classrooms where students' can focus attention on the questions in the left column.

Figure 8.1

Questions That Reveal Students' Understanding of the Purpose of School

Questions Relevant to a Classroom Focused on Learning	Questions Relevant to a Classroom Focused on Compliance
• What specific skill am I trying to improve? • What do I understand already? • What are the important aspects of quality? • What strategies can I apply to produce high-quality work? • How does the feedback inform or affirm my next efforts to improve?	• What is the assignment? • Is this graded? • How many points for each part? • What are the directions/steps I need to follow? • What was my grade?

How do our beliefs about the purpose of school influence our actions?

In their book *Understanding by Design,* Wiggins and McTighe (2005) explain what they call the "twin sins" (p. 3) of curriculum design: coverage without understanding and activities without understanding. The *coverage* approach emphasizes covering a lot of content at the surface level, which results in little or no deep understanding. Think of a classroom on a loop where students march through the textbook each day, answering end-of-unit questions and memorizing long lists of vocabulary words. The *activity* approach emphasizes the completion of projects and activities that may be interesting and engaging but do little to improve students' understanding of prioritized standards. Think of students doing engaging projects or didactic busywork, but neither type of task challenges and supports deep understanding of prioritized standards or demonstrates evidence of shared success criteria. In both cases, students are busy and doing a lot of work, but there is little or no cumulative effect from their efforts to deepen their understanding of anything significant.

The remedy to the twin sins is to first *think like an assessor of understanding.* To better understand what this means and how it's different from an approach that emphasizes content and activities, see Figure 8.2.

Figure 8.2

Three Purposes for School: Teachers' Priorities and Associated Planning Questions

Focus	Purposeful About Learning	Purposeful About Compliance	
	Thinking Like an Assessor of Understanding (Focus on Learning)	Thinking Like an Activity Designer (Focus on Products)	Thinking About Coverage (Focus on Quantity)
Teachers' Metacognitive Planning Questions	How will I clarify for students what evidence of understanding is most important?	What activities would be interesting and engaging?	What needs to be covered before the end of the year?
	How will I intentionally design assessment items/performance tasks to prioritize teaching and learning?	What resources and materials are available?	What media and texts are available on this topic?
	How will I be able to distinguish between those who really understand and those who don't (though they may seem to)?	What activities will students be doing in and out of class? What assignments will be given?	What assignments can be given so I know students have been held accountable for covering content?
	Against what criteria will students and I distinguish the assessment evidence as related to standards?	How will I give students a grade (and justify it to their parents)?	How will I give students a grade (and justify it to their parents)?
	What inferences can I make about learners' progress toward success criteria? What type of feedback can students use to clarify, prioritize, internalize?	Did students follow the directions and complete the activities? Why or why not?	Did students remember the content? Why or why not?

Content in the first and second columns adapted from Wiggins & McTighe, 2005.

All three columns require our attention. However, the column we prioritize becomes the column our students internalize. Consider how a teacher's focus in each area might be articulated to explain his or her purpose for teaching and prioritizing student learning:

- **A Teacher Whose Purpose Is to Cover Content:** "I see my role as presenting content to students. My assumption is that they know the thinking skills and strategies to make meaning of the content I am teaching. There is a lot of content kids need to know, and if I don't cover it with them, they'll never learn it. Every unit is a new 'brick' of content that students will eventually assemble as a wall of understanding."

- **A Teacher Whose Purpose Is to Assign Activities:** "I see my role as giving my students hands-on, engaging activities. My assumption is that they know the thinking skills and strategies to make meaning of the content I am teaching. My primary responsibility is to give them tasks so they can present the content back to me. Sometimes it's a worksheet, sometimes it's a special project or presentation, sometimes it's a group project. Every unit is a new opportunity for projects or activities that will eventually result in understanding."

- **A Teacher Whose Purpose Is to Help Students Think Like Assessors of Understanding:** "I see my role as helping students integrate new knowledge and skills with their existing knowledge and skills. My goal is to support students' efforts to appreciate and understand what high-quality work looks like in this discipline. I want my students to know what is most important to learn, honestly self-assess their current skills and understanding, and then close that gap by using an effective strategy to improve. The most important skills and understandings cannot be taught in a single lesson or even a single unit. Every unit is an additional opportunity to deepen students' understanding of frequently recurring—and intentionally prioritized—content, concepts, and skills."

Only the third approach prioritizes our efforts to clearly and effectively guide students' strategic efforts to learn what it means to understand and what is most important to understand. To further clarify the benefits and consequences of how teachers view their purpose, let's look at how these three purposes prioritize students' efforts to learn.

How do our actions prioritize students' strategic efforts to succeed?

How do students respond to classrooms that emphasize compliance with coverage and activities as compared to those that emphasize learning to demonstrate higher-quality evidence of understanding? If students believe the purpose of school is to learn, they need to be strategic about engaging in a circuitous, recursive process of continuous improvement. This stands in stark contrast to the linear, transactional process that emphasizes compliance as the purpose of schooling (see Figure 8.3).

Figure 8.3

Student Response to a Compliance Environment Versus a Learning Environment

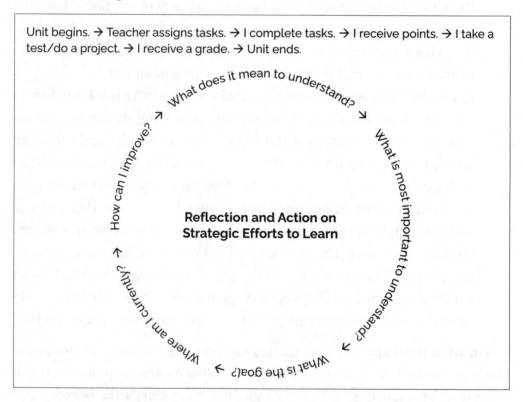

The problem with the linear approach is that it encourages students to be strategically compliant; they see the goal of a unit as completing tasks and attaining points rather than improving and deepening their learning. Compliance is efficient, but it comes at a significant cost. In a national survey of nearly a million U.S. students, only 32 percent of 11th graders report being engaged in school while 34 percent are actively disengaged (Gallup, 2016). A mere 28 percent strongly agree that their schoolwork is important. In some cases, this disengagement results in kids dropping out of school. More often, it results in kids struggling to cope with school. As Denise Clark Pope (2001) explains in her synthesis of interviews conducted while shadowing high school students for a semester,

> They studied the material, read the textbooks, and completed the assignments, for the most part, because they had to, not because they wanted to or because the subjects genuinely interested them. Students often memorized facts and figures without stopping to ask what they meant, or why they were asked to learn the facts in the first place. . . . [One student] said most of the facts she had memorized [were then] 'emptied out of her brain.' She was required to move on to the next assignment to keep up with the pace of class. (pp. 155–156)

Absent a shared purpose for learning, students become strategic about putting forth as little effort as possible to comply with arbitrary expectations. In short, they cope with the clutter. They are compliant in the moment, but they come to expect that much of the content will disappear when a new unit begins. They become strategic about discarding—or outright ignoring— what they see as someone else's clutter. What's the cumulative effect? In our pursuit of getting to the next activity and covering the next chunk of content, students become strategic about forgetting rather than learning.

Unless we are clear about priorities within a discipline and create consensus around what evidence of understanding looks like, students cannot be strategic in their efforts to learn. This isn't a student problem; it's a systems problem. Figure 8.4 is similar to Figure 8.2, which focused on teachers' approaches to teaching like an assessor, activity designer, or content coverer, but now we focus on the cumulative effect of these approaches from the students' perspective.

Consider how these perceptions of the purpose of school might prioritize students' beliefs and action:

- **A Student Whose Purpose Is Compliance to Remember Content:** "I see my role as memorizing the stuff my teacher tells me to. I don't really

Figure 8.4

Three Purposes for School: Students' Priorities and Internal Reflection Questions

Focus	Purposeful About Learning	Purposeful About Compliance (Coping with Clutter)	
	Developing and Demonstrating Understanding (Focus on Learning)	Doing Activities (Focus on Products)	Knowing the Content That Is Covered (Focus on Quantity)
Students' Metacognitive Planning Questions	What is most important to understand in this unit?	What do I have to do to get the most points for this task?	What content do I need to know for the test?
	Where am I now, relative to the skills and understandings in the success criteria and on the exemplars?	When is this due?	When is the test?
	What strategies will help me improve my understanding of the most important content, concepts, and skills?	Am I following the directions necessary to complete the task?	Am I studying the right content/doing the right types of problems that will be on the test?
	How am I doing relative to the success criteria?	What is my final score?	What percentage did I get correct?
	What have I learned? What strategies were useful?	Was the grade fair?	Was the test fair?

understand the big picture, but I know how to get the points and get good grades. Every unit, I do the assignments, take notes, follow the study guide, and study for the next test."

- **A Student Whose Purpose Is Compliance to Complete Activities:** "I see my role as doing my work and following the directions so I can get the most points and best grades. As long as I plan ahead, I can do pretty well on things, follow directions, and get my work done. Every unit, there's a new project/lab/book to do, and I always get it done."

- **A Student Whose Purpose Is to Learn and Demonstrate Evidence of Deep Understanding:** "I see my role as learning new skills and showing my teacher evidence of my understanding. My teacher expects a lot from me. I am always being asked to revise my work and make it better. We use the same success criteria again and again, and every time I think I finally get it, my teacher pushes me a bit further. I can explain how our success criteria, learning goals, and assessment tasks or activities are related. My teacher expects me to respond to feedback, self-assess the quality of my work, and reflect on the strategies I am using to try to improve."

Like the students' in Pope's study, the first two students are compliant but aren't sure how the content or activities connect back to the most important ways of thinking and doing within a discipline. Only the third student is clearly focused on transferrable skills and understandings that can be developed from unit to unit and course to course until they are integrated and internalized as habits of mind.

Shared Purpose: Action Steps

A shared purpose for learning, rather than compliance, can be used to minimize clutter and create clarity for teaching and learning. To establish and use a shared purpose for learning across programs, courses, units, and lessons, use the following action steps:

- Articulate a shared purpose for learning in a standards-based system.
- Align priorities for learning at the system, discipline, course, and unit levels.
- Communicate your priorities and purpose clearly, concisely, and consistently.

Action Step 1

Articulate a shared purpose for learning in a standards-based system. Establishing a shared purpose for learning in a standards-based system can be accomplished by asking four questions aligned to purpose, vision, commitments, and priorities (and then synthesizing the responses). The first three questions create clarity at the systems level, whereas the fourth does so at the discipline or department level:

- Why do we exist? This will help determine and articulate the shared purpose of your system.
- When students graduate, what do we want them to be like? This will help determine and articulate your vision of a successful learner in your system.
- To fulfill our purpose and support our vision, how should we prioritize our efforts to prioritize students' strategic efforts to learn? This will help determine and articulate your shared commitments to support learners.
- Why is it important that students take classes in this discipline? This will help determine and articulate your priorities for learning in each discipline. This is also a question to ask at the department level before going through the process described in Chapter 4 to identify priority standards.

Once these responses have been gathered, synthesized, and refined, they should be published. These statements of shared purpose (see sample purpose statement in Figure 8.6, p. 145) can be used at the school and department levels as criteria to provide clarity—and minimize clutter—when making important decisions related to curriculum, instruction, and assessment.

Action Step 2

Align priorities for learning at the system, discipline, course, and unit levels. If we want our students to internalize our shared purpose for learning, we need a shared language that helps us describe and align the most important elements in that system. Without a shared meaning of important terms, clear communication and aligned actions are not possible. For example, we can't prioritize students' efforts related to *learning goals* if, throughout the day, they hear them referred to as a *learning goal, learning target, learning objective,* and *learning outcome*—or if they are not referred to at all. Shared language creates clarity.

Consider the following terms related to *what it means to understand* and *what is important to understand* that have been described in this book. They can be used to create shared constraints to establish important elements in a systems-level approach to clarity. They should appear frequently in curriculum guides, course syllabi, unit and lesson overviews, and assessments. Feel free to use other specific terms or establish your own definitions. What matters is that a limited number of terms are identified, definitions are established, and the meanings are shared.

- **What It Means to Understand**: *general scale for success criteria, shared success criteria, shared language of assessment, task, prompt, directions, surface-level knowledge, deep understanding, aligned evidence*
- **What Is Most Important to Understand:** *priority standards, enduring understandings, essential questions, basic academic terms, complex academic terms, priority skills, disciplinary concepts, learning goal*

First, teachers use this shared language to establish shared constraints and minimize clutter as they identify priorities for learning at the program or department level. Then those priorities are used to create course overviews, which are used to create instructional units, which are used to plan daily lessons.

Once you've established a shared purpose (as described above) and identified priority standards that are aligned to a shared scale for success criteria (as discussed in Chapter 4), departments and teacher teams can identify, articulate, and align discipline, course, and unit priorities. This is not something casually done on a professional development day or across a series of 30-minute team meetings; it is a process that needs to be done strategically over an extended period of time (see Figure 8.5).

Note that, once established, the system- and discipline-level priorities are used *verbatim* at the course, unit, and lesson levels. Only the specific academic content and skills change across courses, units, and lessons. When this is done with fidelity, it eliminates clutter and addresses the root cause of the clarity paradox. We've discarded the plethora of arbitrarily worded and differently formatted rubrics, scales, success criteria, unit overviews, and so on. Our shared purpose and priorities are aligned and can be seen with clarity.

Figure 8.5

Flow of Priority Levels

System-Level Priorities (established by all staff):
- shared purpose
- general scale for success criteria
- common language of assessment

Discipline-Level Priorities (established by department *and aligned to system priorities*):
- priority standards
- shared success criteria and general assessment prompts aligned to general scale for success criteria
- disciplinary concepts
- enduring understandings
- essential questions

Course-Level Priorities (established by teacher teams *and aligned to specific discipline-level priorities*):
- priority standards
- shared success criteria
- aligned academic content, concepts, and skills
- learning goals
- aligned assessment prompts

Unit-Level Priorities (established by individual teachers or teacher teams *and aligned to discipline and course priorities*):
- most important learning goals, academic content, terms, and skills

Lesson-Level Priorities (established by individual teachers *and aligned to discipline, course, and unit priorities*):
- learning goal as aligned to the specific task and shared success criteria

Action Step 3

Communicate your priorities and purpose clearly, concisely, and consistently. Once priorities for learning in disciplines and courses have been established and aligned, they need to be communicated in clear, concise, and consistent ways with students. For a useful metaphor in thinking about how a complex system can be designed and communicated in a manner that is clear and accessible for users, consider your smartphone.

Your smartphone is a remarkable tool. It allows you to access information, communicate with others, organize your life, take photos, and more. Its tools are easily accessible because of the design of the operating system (OS) and an easy-to-use display. Designers established nonnegotiable constraints to establish a uniform look for the icons, organize the layout, and determine the functionality of the buttons and swiping motions to ensure the phone is easy to use. Behind the screens and icons are millions of lines of computer code—which you do not see—written by programmers who also adhered to nonnegotiable constraints that guided their use of a shared programming language to make the OS work as intended.

Because of these shared constraints, users can access the functionality of the phone with maximal autonomy. A good OS minimizes extraneous cognitive load. Open your phone, and you can clearly focus on the distinct, prioritized elements. The icons and apps are concise; they are intentionally designed to communicate as much meaningful information as possible with as few words as necessary. The interface is consistent; you know exactly how your icons will be arranged and how they will look the next time you open your phone. The clarity, conciseness, and consistency are what make it useful.

Now think about the frustration you feel when there is a major OS update or when you get a new phone with a different OS. Minor differences in layout, icon design, and the actions related to selecting and swiping eliminate the consistency, and you suddenly need to muddle through what had been familiar and easy to use. After several days, you learn the new system and build fluency, but what if the OS kept changing? How useful would your phone be if the layout, icons, apps, and rules for sliding and swiping changed every few weeks? What if they changed every 52 minutes?

Unfortunately, this is what the clutter of expectations and formatting in syllabi, textbooks, rubrics, assignments, and assessments can look like through students' eyes. As they move from grade to grade, course to course, unit to unit, and lesson to lesson, there is little continuity in how to understand and access the functionality of the system. Teachers may know the lines of code, but there is not a predictable interface that students can use to navigate the OS. What is your school's OS? What are the clear, concise, and consistent ways you help students identify and navigate the priorities that have been identified for each discipline, course, unit, and lesson?

Let's look at how a shared purpose and an aligned OS could be communicated (Figure 8.6). At first glance, it looks like a traditional, philosophical statement of purpose. But look more closely, and it reads more like a getting started guide for how to navigate the system's OS. Not only does it describe a shared purpose, it also describes how priorities related to *what it means to understand* and *what is most important to understand* will be communicated clearly, concisely, and consistently across the entire system so they are accessible and useful to students.

Now that the form and function of the important components of the system have been established, templates can be used to clearly, concisely, and consistently communicate the alignment of purpose and priorities at the program, course, unit, and lesson levels.

A program overview would describe priorities and shared purpose for the school or district's reading, mathematics, or physical education program. A template would include elements articulated in the system- and discipline-level priorities, and—depending on the grade span and discipline—the overview may run from several to dozens of pages. For example, programs that are allocated more instructional time will be longer than those that are allocated less instructional time.

Figure 8.7 shows an example of a template that could be used to clearly, concisely, and consistently communicate priorities for a course. Notice that the elements with an asterisk have already been established at the program level because they represent prioritized, transferable skills and understandings and are repeated frequently across courses within a given discipline.

Figure 8.6

Example of a Systems-Level Statement of Purpose and Shared Focus

What is our shared purpose?

The purpose of curriculum, instruction, and assessment in our district is to develop each student's skills and abilities to demonstrate evidence of deep understanding related to priority standards as aligned to our shared success criteria. To these ends, we will support students' strategic efforts to strive to produce high-quality work, ask thought-provoking questions, persevere when faced with challenges, work collaboratively to solve important problems, and be responsive to opportunities to learn.

What does it mean to understand?

Understanding is a process in which a learner acquires skills and knowledge with enough depth to transfer those understandings to new topics, concepts, or contexts. We've identified a **General Scale for Success Criteria** to communicate different levels of understanding across all programs and classes.

This shared scale is used to guide our strategic efforts to develop students' skills and understanding. It is the basis for assessment design, unit and lesson planning, feedback, and grading.

Beginning	Approaching	Proficient	Advanced
I can define terms or follow simple procedures.	I can describe or combine terms and follow multistep procedures.	I can connect, compare, and explain relationships between content and concepts or strategically engage in complex procedures.	I can transfer skills and understandings to new topics, concepts, or contexts to engage in, and reflect on my approach to strategizing and solving authentic, novel problems.

What is most important to understand?

The most important understandings in any discipline are those that can be transferred across lessons, units, courses, and programs into authentic settings. These understandings are then used by learners to make deeper meaning of content, concepts, strategies, and skills. Within each discipline, we focus on a manageable number of these **Priority Standards** (typically 5 to 8) that have been aligned across the four levels of our General Scale as standards-aligned **Shared Success Criteria**.

If there are different elements already in place in your school or district, you can also establish your own template. What matters is the clarity, conciseness, and consistency with which it is used to communicate what is most important to understand and what it means to understand. For example, I am a huge advocate of developing and using essential questions and enduring understandings, as explained by Wiggins and McTighe (2005). Notice that I've placed them at the discipline level as aligned to priority standards. This way, they can be transferred from course to course and, with minor

Figure 8.7

Example of a Course Overview Template

Course Title:				
Purpose Statement for the Course:				
Priority Content Standards*		**Essential Questions***	**Enduring Understandings***	
(5–8 rows by category)		*(5–8 aligned EQs)*	*(5–8 aligned EUs)*	
Central Concepts*				
(8–12 central concepts)		*(definitions of concepts)*		
Shared Language of Assessment*				
(8–10 assessment terms)		*(definitions of assessment terms)*		
Units of Study – Link Content to Priority Standard				
(titles of each unit should link to a content standard and a priority standard)				
Priority Standards Aligned to Success Criteria*				
Priority Standard	**Beginning**	**Approaching**	**Proficient**	**Advanced**
(5–8 priority standards aligned to shared success criteria)				
Priority Standard Areas Aligned to Shared Success Criteria, Learning Goals, Prompts* *(Approximately 2 standards per page for elementary priority standards; 1 per page for middle and high school priority standards)*				
Level of Evidence	**Beginning**	**Approaching**	**Proficient**	**Advanced**
Shared Success Criteria				
Aligned Learning Goals				
Aligned Assessment Prompts/Tasks				

modification of semantics, from unit to unit. However, if new essential questions and enduring understandings are developed for every new lesson, as I've mistakenly seen them utilized, they are neither essential nor enduring and may simply be creating clutter.

An example of a common template for a unit overview is shown in Figure 8.8. Notice that many of the elements (as noted by an asterisk) have already been established at the program and course levels. Though the specific content and skills change from unit to unit, the prioritized elements are transferable and recursive.

Figure 8.8

Example of a Unit Overview Template

Who Had Power and How Was It Used? Explaining Cause and Effect in the Civil Rights Era				
Content/Terms Important to Understand in this Unit				
More Basic Content/Terms			More Complex Content/Terms	
Dwight D. Eisenhower, John F. Kennedy, Little Rock Nine (1957), Lyndon B. Johnson, Malcolm X, Martin Luther King, Jr., March on Washington (1963), Montgomery Bus Boycott (1955–1956), Rosa Parks, Southern Christian Leadership Conference, Thurgood Marshall			*Brown v. Board of Education* (1957), civil disobedience, Civil Rights Act of 1964, *de facto, de jure,* Fair Housing Act of 1968, Jim Crow, poll tax, segregation, Selma to Montgomery Marches (1965), Voting Rights Act of 1965	
Disciplinary Concepts Important to Understand in this Unit*				
justice	*power*	*authority*	*stability and change*	*cause and effect*
Shared Assessment Language Important to Demonstrate Understanding in this Unit*				
define	*describe*	*develop*	*explain*	*contextualize*
Content Standards for Historical Reasoning and Political Science Important to this Unit*				
Cause and Effect: Uses multiple perspectives to analyze and explain the causes and effects of issues or events within and across time periods, events, or cultures				
Civil Rights and Civil Liberties: Describes the evolution of rights over time including key laws, constitutional changes, court decisions and how collective action movements work to extend rights.				

continued

Figure 8.8 *(continued)*

Example of a Unit Overview Template

Priority Standard Area and Aligned Learning Goals and Assessment Prompts in this Unit				
	Beginning	**Developing**	**Proficient**	**Advanced**
Standard Area: Construct Written Explanations in History*	Accurately states important facts and relevant details as related to a historical topic.	Accurately identifies relevant facts and important details to describe or summarize the historical relevance of decisions, actions, or events.	Organizes information to develop accurate explanations about the relationship among individuals, decisions, and events by providing historical context and using relevant facts, details, quotations, or examples.	Develops and contextualizes accurate, detailed explanations about relationships among historically relevant individuals, decisions, or events using important facts, relevant details, well-chosen quotations, and nuanced examples and counter-examples.
Aligned Learning Goals*	I can identify relevant individuals, decisions, or events as related to a period in history.	• I can state who, what, where, why, when, and how as related to a historically relevant decision, action, or event. • I can summarize using relevant facts and important details.	• I can describe important relationships among events/concepts/individuals/decisions. • I can clarify a concept or explanation with relevant examples and non-examples.	• I can develop and organize clear explanations about causal relationships among historically relevant individuals, decisions, or events. • I can clarify an explanation with a well-chosen, contextualized, relevant detail or quotation. • I can hypothesize and justify a "What if?" scenario.

	Beginning	Developing	Proficient	Advanced
Aligned Assessment Prompts (Explanations / Cause and Effect)*	• Who did/ was…? • What happened? • When did it happen? • Where did it happen?	• Who did what, when? • Why did…? • How did…? • What else?	• What are the relationships among the main components? • What is a relevant example or non-example? • What are the important details? • What concepts connect details to big ideas? • Explain why, how…	• What else was happening during this time that was relevant to provide context? • What was the initial cause and the ultimate effect? How do we know? • What additional relationships or details are important for a nuanced understanding?

* Denotes components established at the discipline-level that are used across multiple courses and units.

Once these elements are in place, teachers can be given autonomy to make decisions about daily lessons, align specific assessment tasks and prompts to shared success criteria, establish learning goals, and plan specific learning activities. As discussed in Chapter 2, we've embraced a chaordic system with minimal structure and maximal autonomy through prioritized constraints. By committing to a shared purpose—and agreeing to what it means to understand and what is most important to understand—we can create clear alignment from system-level priorities to daily learning goals.

Learning goals establish a shared purpose for teaching and learning a lesson (see Marzano, 2007 or Moss & Brookhart, 2012 for detailed explanations). They answer, "What is our priority for where we should invest our strategic effort for learning today?" Learning goals are derived from standards and clarify—for teachers and students—the important knowledge, understandings, or skills that will be developed by participating in a lesson. (Examples of this alignment were presented in Figure 5.2). They are stated in terms of what will be learned (e.g., "Identify and summarize important components of the 1965 Voting Rights Act") and are distinct from, but must be aligned to, the task (e.g., "Read pages 253–264 and answer the questions provided").

The importance of the function of learning goals to prioritize teachers' and students' efforts cannot be overstated. In fact, all the elements of clarity we've developed thus far are meaningless unless they are used to establish a clear purpose for teaching and learning for each lesson. Learning goals help teachers intentionally design assessment tasks, plan lessons responsive to students' learning needs, and provide a focal point for meaningful feedback to scaffold students to deeper levels of understanding. Most powerfully, learning goals are used by students to help them prioritize their attention and effort as they plan, monitor, and evaluate the effectiveness of the strategies they use to learn.

In systems that haven't clearly identified a shared purpose for learning, a shared language of assessment, or a shared scale for success criteria, learning goals may be seen as irrelevant, devoid of meaning, or just more clutter. These critiques are logically sound, but they are indictments of a failure to prioritize and establish a shared purpose for learning rather than an indictment of learning goals specifically.

Fortunately, in a system that has established and articulated priorities for learning across programs, courses, and units, establishing learning goals is a straightforward process. If you think of a unit overview as a map of the important territory for a unit, then a learning goal describes the destination for the day. To establish clear learning goals

- Identify the important standards and academic content that will be the focus of the day's lesson.
- Identify relevant reasoning skills as aligned to the success criteria.
- State the relationship between the content and the reasoning skill as aligned to the shared success criteria.
- Communicate the learning goal in a manner that can be used by the teacher and learner to prioritize their strategic efforts to learn.

To communicate learning goals to these ends, we turn back to the three questions we initially used to establish clarity at the systems level. Now we use adaptations of those questions to focus students' attention on the purpose of the day's lesson:

- What does it mean to understand? *State the success criteria.*
- What is most important to understand? *State the learning goal of today's lesson.*
- How do we prioritize our strategic effort to help students understand what is most important? *State the aligned task used to develop and demonstrate understanding.*

At a minimum, the learning goal should be visible to students and referenced throughout the lesson. Even more powerfully, all three of these elements can be presented in reverse order by identifying the task, learning goal, and success criteria. They can be presented as a bulleted list or by using a sentence frame as follows:

> [*Do task*] so you can [*learning goal*] in a manner that [*success criteria*].

Applying this frame to the unit template from Figure 8.8, alignment among these three elements could be articulated as follows:

> Read pages 253–264 and answer the questions provided so you can identify and summarize important components of the 1965 Voting Rights Act in a manner that accurately identifies relevant facts and important details to describe or summarize the historical relevance of decisions, actions, or events.

Clearly, the articulation of these three components would be shorter for younger students. Keep in mind that the full text of the success criteria wouldn't need to be fully written out. For example, as students build familiarity with the success criteria, the relevant portion of the success criteria could just be referenced as "See success criteria for 'Developing' for 'Written Explanations.'"

When something is purposeful, it is relevant to a specific goal and strategically useful. In a standards-based system, the purpose of schools is to prioritize each student's strategic efforts to learn clearly articulated standards. By clearly aligning and communicating priorities for learning at the system, discipline, course, and unit levels, we clarify a shared purpose for learning rather than compliance. By communicating clear learning goals for lessons that are aligned to consistently recurring priority standards and shared success criteria, we help students prioritize their strategic efforts to learn. For a summary of important ideas and strategies discussed in this chapter, see Figure 8.9.

Shared Purpose: Revisiting the Scenarios

In the first scenario (For Thursday, complete p. 349, 1–23 odds; On Friday, test), from the distribution of the syllabus onward, the class is about coverage and compliance. The course is driven by rules and procedures, and there seems to be very little time or attention given to the Mathematics Practice Standards—or to any disciplinary concepts.

In the second scenario (Developing clarity of purpose; developing deeper understanding), the class is focused on a shared purpose of improving learning. Tasks and activities are seen as a means to an end of building fluency and deepening understanding in the most important ways of thinking and doing in mathematics. Students still learn computations and operations, but they engage in much more—and much deeper—thinking, reasoning, and meaning-making. Students are clear about what is important to understand in the program, the course, and each unit. They are also clear about how tasks and assignments prioritize their efforts to learn. They are given time to use meaningful feedback to improve, are given opportunities to be metacognitive about their understanding, and are reflective about their use of strategies to learn.

Shared Purpose: Questions for Discussion and Reflection

- How do I/we clarify for students that our shared purpose is to improve learning?
- How do I/we clearly, concisely, and consistently communicate to students what evidence of understanding is most important in each discipline, course, unit, and lesson?
- If components described in this chapter were implemented in our school/district, how might teachers and students benefit after a few years of consistent efforts to use them to prioritize students' strategic efforts to learn?

Figure 8.9

Shared Purpose: Avoiding Clutter, Minimizing the Clarity Paradox, and Choosing Clarity

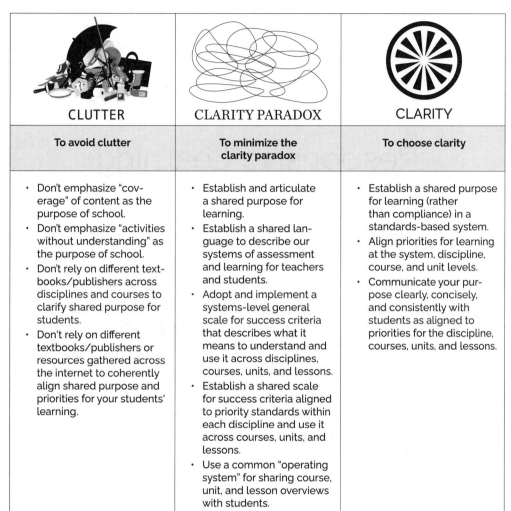

CLUTTER	CLARITY PARADOX	CLARITY
To avoid clutter	**To minimize the clarity paradox**	**To choose clarity**
• Don't emphasize "coverage" of content as the purpose of school. • Don't emphasize "activities without understanding" as the purpose of school. • Don't rely on different textbooks/publishers across disciplines and courses to clarify shared purpose for students. • Don't rely on different textbooks/publishers or resources gathered across the internet to coherently align shared purpose and priorities for your students' learning.	• Establish and articulate a shared purpose for learning. • Establish a shared language to describe our systems of assessment and learning for teachers and students. • Adopt and implement a systems-level general scale for success criteria that describes what it means to understand and use it across disciplines, courses, units, and lessons. • Establish a shared scale for success criteria aligned to priority standards within each discipline and use it across courses, units, and lessons. • Use a common "operating system" for sharing course, unit, and lesson overviews with students.	• Establish a shared purpose for learning (rather than compliance) in a standards-based system. • Align priorities for learning at the system, discipline, course, and unit levels. • Communicate your purpose clearly, concisely, and consistently with students as aligned to priorities for the discipline, courses, units, and lessons.

9

Responsive Learning

How do students' beliefs about ability, strategy, and effort affect how they respond to different opportunities to learn? As you consider this question in the following scenarios, you'll notice they are much longer than those used in the previous chapters. These two scenarios incorporate each of the elements of clarity discussed throughout this book. They've been written to position you to empathize with your students as novices trying to learn a new, complex set of skills. To make this possible, the scenarios intentionally focus on a skill set with which you are familiar but is (probably) outside the realm of what you've formally taught or learned: stand-up comedy. As you read, notice how the alignment and presence (or misalignment and absence) of focused success criteria, intentional design of assessments, reliability of inferences about evidence of understanding, meaningful feedback, and a shared purpose for learning support (or undermine) how students respond to the opportunity to learn.

Non-Exemplar: The unresponsive path to learned helplessness. You have enrolled in a high school course about stand-up comedy. On the first day of class, you are told that at the end of the course, you will have to do a performance assessment consisting of a three-minute comedy routine for your classmates. Even though it is months away, you are anxious about performing your routine. "Being funny" is something that people often attribute to innate ability, and you don't think you've got it. A few weeks into the class, you find that you are really enjoying it and you like your teacher. You read about different stand-up comedians, watch classic routines and discuss them with classmates, and write a research paper on your favorite comedian. With a couple weeks left in class, you are given the instructions for the performance assessment:

- **Assignment/Task:** Give an original three-minute stand-up comedy routine on topics of your choice to the class.
- **Goal:** Give a very funny stand-up comedy routine demonstrating what you've learned.
- **Success Criteria:** See Stand-Up Comedy Rubric (Figure 9.1).

Figure 9.1

Success Criteria for Stand-Up Comedy Performance Task (Non-Exemplar)

	1	2	3	4
Number of Jokes	0 jokes	1–3 jokes	4–6 jokes	7 or more jokes
Number of Topics	1 topic	2 topics	3 topics	4 topics
Creativity	Demonstrates wonderful, creative insights and a vivid imagination	Demonstrates marvelous, deep creative thinking and openness to new ideas	Demonstrates amazing levels of creative expression and meets expectations of openness to new, creative ideas	The creative thinking is extremely profound and exceeds all expectations of creative wonderment
Level of Humor	Not funny	Somewhat funny	Funny	Very funny

You design your routine and use the success criteria as your guide. You cover several topics, have nine jokes, and think your routine is very creative. However, when you give the routine, it goes horribly. A few classmates crack a smile, but no one laughs. Your teacher gives you the rubric back with specific judgmental feedback. She's given you a 3 for Number of Jokes ("Apparently, she missed some," you think to yourself), a 3 for Number of Topics, and a 2 for both Creativity and Level of Humor.

Beneath the rubric, she writes the following comment: "Good job! But I really need you to try to be funnier. If you want to revise your routine, you can do it again next week." You are disappointed, but deep down you know the teacher is right. In fact, you think the 2 for Level of Humor was really a gift; your routine wasn't funny. After class the next day, you tell your teacher you'd like to revise and redo your routine. She looks you in the eye and says, "I believe in you; you really have a lot of potential. The reason I gave you a 2 for creativity is because my expectations are so high for you!"

You spend the next few days working harder than ever on your routine. You add more jokes and are up to 12 now. You add two more topics for a grand total of five, and they are exceptionally creative. Later that week, you give your routine again. It is the longest three minutes of your life. Despite your revisions, no one even cracks a smile. By the end of the routine, you feel like there is no oxygen in the room. You feel defeated.

You get your rubric back. This time, your teacher has given you another 3 for Number of Jokes ("I guess she's missing them because I'm not funny," you think to yourself), a 4 for Number of Topics, a 3 for Creativity, and a 2.5 for Level of Humor. Beneath the rubric, she writes, "Good job! You've added a lot to this! You've definitely added more creative topics and it was funnier! I'll revise your score."

Despite her kindness, you know it wasn't funny. In fact, this proves what you already feared: you aren't funny. You tried even harder and somehow your routine was even worse. As you walk to your next class, the voice in your head quietly whispers, "I knew I wasn't funny; I'm just not as talented as the other people in the class."

Exemplar: How alignment supports a thriving response. The teacher in the previous scenario has the opportunity to revise her course. First, she identifies priority standards and shared success criteria. She identifies five transferrable standards for writing and delivering a stand-up comedy routine:

- **Has an Awareness of the Audience:** Comedians present material that is relevant and relatable to their audience.

- **Establishes Premise:** Comedy is based on a premise in which the audience sees themselves—a situation familiar to the audience or an absurd situation the audience can clearly imagine.
- **Delivers Payoff or Punchline:** It's called a punchline because you don't see it coming and the surprise invokes a physical response. The payoff is related to the amount of time spent building expectations only to surprise the audience with an absurd, unexpected, or benign resolution.
- **Applies Comedic Principles:** Although comedic topics are specifically cultural, the structure of *how* different types of jokes are designed is nearly universal. The most frequently used structures are based on principles of convergence, incongruity, and callback.
- **Delivers Jokes Effectively:** Comedians are most effective when their delivery is authentic, they are fully committed to the premise, and they believe the payoff is worth the audience's time. Comedians use tone, volume, and timing to keep the audience engaged and give them enough time to process the premise and punchline.

The teacher then aligns the priority standards to the school's shared scale for success criteria (Figure 9.2). As she looks at the new prioritized standards and shared success criteria, she realizes there were many opportunities in the previous version of the course to prepare students for the performance task. She realizes she can continue to have students watch and discuss routines, read about specific comedians, and write about their favorite comedians, but students need to do those things with a purpose. The purpose of all of that watching, reading, writing, and discussing is to build an understanding of how to think like a comedian. From the first day of the revised course, the success criteria are used by students to understand and analyze how and why comedians do what they do.

Next, the teacher aligns learning goals to the priority standards and success criteria. She realizes there are specific learning goals aligned to each standard area and each level of success criteria. The learning goals for the course are now remarkably clear; levels of learning goals 1–4 are aligned to the unistructural, multistructural, relational, and extended abstract levels of the success criteria along the school's 4-point scale.

Figure 9.2

Learning Goals Aligned to Priority Standards and Shared Success Criteria for Stand-up Comedy (Exemplar)

Standard Area	1	2	3	4
Has an Awareness of the Audience	I can define and give examples of basic terms related to audience awareness.	• When watching routines, I can identify and describe how the comedian demonstrates awareness of the audience. • When writing jokes or a routine, I can describe relevant attributes of the audience.	• When watching routines, I can explain how material was topical, relevant, or relatable to the audience. • When writing jokes, I can identify and explain the background knowledge required of the audience.	When writing a routine, I can identify, explain, and justify how the material is relevant and relatable to the audience.
Establishes Premise	I can define and give examples of basic terms related to establishing a premise.	• When watching routines, I can identify and describe the premise of different jokes or portions of the routine. • Given a premise, I can write a punchline.	• When watching routines, I can explain why the premise appeared to be effective or ineffective. • I can write a joke with a premise relatable to the target audience.	When writing a routine, I can explain and justify how the material is relevant and relatable to the audience.
Payoff or Punchline	I can define and give examples of basic terms related to payoffs and punchline.	• When watching routines, I can identify and describe the intent of the payoff and punchline. • Given a punchline, I can write a premise.	• When watching routines, I can explain why the payoff or punchline was worth—or not worth—the set-up time. • I can write a joke with a payoff or punchline that is not obvious but aligned to the premise.	When writing a routine, I can explain and justify how the payoffs or punchlines are absurd, benign, or violate the expectation of the premise.

Applies Comedic Principles	I can define and give examples of basic terms related to the comedic principles of convergence, incongruity, and callback.	• When watching routines, I can identify and describe components of convergence, incongruity, and callback. • Given a comedic principle and a premise, I can write a joke based on that principle.	• When watching routines, I can explain how comedians use convergence, incongruity, and callback for comedic effect. • I can write original jokes based on the comedic principles of convergence, incongruity, and callback.	When writing an original routine, I can develop and combine sequences of jokes that apply the comedic principles of convergence, incongruity, and callback across the routine.
Delivers Jokes or Comedy Routines Effectively	I can define and give examples of basic terms related to the elements of effective delivery, including fluency, tone, engaging, processing, and responding.	When watching routines, I can identify and describe when and how the comedian is using tone, volume, silence, or wait time.	• When watching routines, I can explain how comedians utilize tone, volume, or wait time to meet audience needs for engaging, processing, and responding. • I can deliver a joke effectively through the appropriate use of tone, volume, silence, and wait time.	• I can fluently deliver an original comedy routine. • I can explain how the choices I made in using tone, volume, pacing, and wait time were suited to the audience's needs for engaging, processing, and responding.

As the teacher looks at these learning goals and how they are aligned directly to the success criteria, she realizes that she needs more intentionally designed tasks across the entire course. Consequently, she revises prompts and performance tasks to ensure students have an opportunity to learn the vocabulary, skills, and strategies aligned to the most important evidence articulated in the learning goals and priority standards.

For example, rather than "do a report" about a comedian, students develop an understanding of priority standards by explaining how different comedians demonstrate audience awareness and use pacing, pauses, and wait time to give the audience the opportunity to respond. Rather than write jokes as a disconnected culminating activity, students learn how to identify, describe, and explain how jokes are based on different comedic principles to align the premise to the punchline across the entire course. Rather than "talk about routines" based on personal preferences, students identify, describe, and explain elements of routines based on specific, discipline-based vocabulary and then analyze those routines based on their shared scale for success criteria.

The shared scale for success criteria is not merely used to judge students on culminating projects as the teacher has done in the past; instead, it is the basis for feedback, self-assessment, and self-reflection that students can use in meaningful ways throughout the entire course to "scaffold up" to deeper levels of understanding.

The final performance assessment is also revised:

- **Assignment/Task:** Give an original three-minute stand-up comedy routine on topics of your choice to the class.
- **Goal:** Develop an original routine based on the comedic principles of convergence, incongruity, and callback that demonstrates attention to audience awareness, has relevant and relatable premises, and is aligned to a payoff or punchline.
- **Success Criteria:** See success criteria in Stand-Up Comedy Rubric (Figure 9.3).

As she thinks about the revisions she's made to the course, the teacher realizes that in the previous iteration, students could be compliant as they covered content and completed projects, but she hadn't spent much time helping students apply transferable strategies that built their capacity to *think like a comedian*. She's eager to teach the revised course to see how students will respond to the new, better-aligned opportunities to learn.

Responsive Learning

Effective teachers are proactively responsive to their students' needs as learners. They know how to use the right strategy, in the right way, at the right time to prioritize their students' strategic efforts to learn. In these

Figure 9.3

Prioritized Standards and Aligned Learning Goals for Stand-Up Comedy Performance Task (Exemplar)

	1	2	3	4
Has an Awareness of the Audience	Can define and give an example of audience awareness	Can describe general information about the target audience	Material is topical and relevant, and scenarios are relatable to most of the target audience	Material is topical and relevant to audience background knowledge and experience; demonstrates awareness of social norms
Establishes Premise	Can define and give an example of premise	Can describe a situation with a premise that is relatable to the audience	Premise is identifiable and relatable to the target audience	Establishes premise, or set-up, that is relevant and relatable to the audience and invokes a logical, emotional, or empathetic response
Delivers Payoff or Punchline	Can define and give an example of payoff or punchline	Can describe typical outcomes of the premise	Payoff or punchline is not obvious but is still aligned to the premise	Fulfills expectation with appropriately absurd or benign payoff or punchline that violates the expectation of the premise or provides relief of tension or anxiety
Applies Comedic Principles	Can define and give an example of convergence, incongruity, and callback	Can describe the components of convergence, incongruity, or callback	Elements of comedic principles are present and identifiable	Uses elements of comedic principles with attention to comparison or juxtaposition between/among the obvious, ordinary, unique, unexpected, or absurd

continued

Figure 9.3 *(continued)*

Prioritized Standards and Aligned Learning Goals for Stand-Up Comedy Performance Task (Exemplar)

	1	2	3	4
Delivers Jokes Effectively	Can define each element of effective delivery, including fluency, tone, and pacing	Tone and volume support the audience's ability to participate; delivery is fluent but inflexible to audience response	Delivery is fluent and uses appropriate tone and volume; shows attention to pacing based on audience response	Demonstrates authenticity and commitment to the delivery through intentional use of tone and volume; is attuned to timing through the use of pacing, pauses, and silence to meet audience needs for engaging, processing, and responding

teachers' classrooms, students are responsive to opportunities to learn in productive ways because they believe they have the ability to accomplish tasks through strategic effort. These students know what an attainable, high-quality performance looks like, and they plan, monitor, and evaluate the quality of their work and the effectiveness of their strategies to improve.

Before students choose how to respond to an opportunity to learn, they quietly ask themselves a simple question: "If I try to do this, will I be successful?" How students answer this question depends on their beliefs about the relationships among ability, effort, strategy, and success. Consider how different students might articulate these beliefs:

- If I don't believe I have the ability to be successful, there is little reason to invest effort in responding to an opportunity to learn.
- If I believe I have the ability to be successful and invest a lot of time and effort doing what my teacher asks but am not successful, I may begin to doubt my ability and become less responsive in the future.
- Even if I don't believe I have the ability to be successful right now, if I believe in my ability to prioritize my efforts to use strategies that help

me be successful, I'll be receptive to current and even more challenging opportunities to learn in the future.

All these statements are logically sound, but only the third statement aligns teachers' and students' strategic efforts to learn. To better understand how the complex relationships among ability, effort, and strategy can inhibit or accelerate one's response to opportunities to learn, consider the divergent paths of learned helplessness and expert performance.

Suppose you are given a complex task. You try the task several times and are not successful. You internalize your failed attempts as evidence of a lack of ability. You grow frustrated and ask a friend for help. Your friend tells you the task is simple; you just aren't trying hard enough. You try again and are still unsuccessful. Completely frustrated, you give up. A week later, you are confronted with the same problem. This time, you don't even bother trying.

Rather than learning how to accomplish the task, the lesson you've (mistakenly) learned is that you are incapable of doing the task. When a learner's effort becomes disconnected from results, this rational—but devastating— response is called learned helplessness (Maier & Seligman, 2016; Seligman & Maier, 1967). The failure to complete the initial task wasn't due to your lack of effort or innate ability. The failure was because you didn't use a strategy that aligned your effort and your current ability to the most important elements of the task. When our interventions to support learning emphasize "Add more!" or "Try harder!" as a response, it assumes the individual already has the strategies and skills required to be successful but has simply chosen not to put forth the effort. In reality, this is rarely the case.

In contrast to the helpless response, consider the expert response (Ericsson, 2006; Ericsson, Krampe, & Tesch-Romer, 1993). Experts apply the right strategy, in the right way, at the right time to attain desired results. Experts prioritize and align their efforts to apply strategies that help them improve in the most important skills. They embrace mistakes as feedback to slow down and modify their approach to apply even more strategic efforts to learn. "Generally, the [expert's] solution is not 'try harder' but rather 'try differently'" (Ericsson & Pool, 2016, p. 19). What they 'try differently' are the specific, deliberate strategies they use to improve.

Consider the effort and strategy used by the student in the stand-up comedy course at the beginning of this chapter. In the first case, the student focused on cluttered, irrelevant success criteria to comply with project requirements. The student's efforts to pursue irrelevant success criteria resulted in the high effort and poor results that are the shortest route to learned helplessness. Had the same student taken the course after the revisions, he or she would have been given the opportunity to observe, practice, and apply the most important knowledge, skills, and strategies in increasingly complex and sophisticated ways to internalize powerful strategies to improve.

Ironically, a hallmark of expert performance is that experts become so adept at transferring strategies to new contexts that they are able to apply less effort, to less information, with more strategic efficiency, to obtain exceptional results (Ericsson & Pool, 2016). Unfortunately, when novices watch an expert in action, they tend to misinterpret the source of the expert's fluency. Because novices rarely have the opportunity to watch the deliberate, strategic effort that experts put forth to develop fluency, they mistakenly attribute the expert's skills to natural ability.

To understand how students' beliefs about ability, strategy, and effort influence their responsiveness to opportunities to learn, we need to consider three questions:

- How do students' beliefs about their ability, strategy, and effort influence their responsiveness to opportunities to learn?
- How do students' beliefs about others' abilities, strategies, and effort influence their responsiveness to opportunities to learn?
- How do effective teachers protect and develop each student's ability to prioritize strategic efforts to learn?

How do students' beliefs about their ability, strategy, and effort influence their responsiveness to opportunities to learn?

Carol Dweck (2000, 2006, 2007, 2010) has spent her career trying to better understand how individuals' beliefs about their abilities affect their results. Individuals who believe they can improve with effort and strategy have what Dweck calls a growth mindset. Individuals who believe they have fixed, inborn abilities and there is little that can be done to improve them have a fixed mindset.

Whether a student has a fixed or a growth mindset has a profound impact on how students respond to opportunities to learn. When a student with a growth mindset is given an opportunity to learn, that student is likely to engage in a thriving response—an alignment of strategy and effort that helps the student improve. However, if the student has a fixed mindset, he or she is likely to adopt a coping response to deal with a perceived inability to improve. What we may see as apathy or laziness is actually a student's rational defense to experiencing failure—going out of their way to avoid being exposed as having low ability. Figure 9.4 shows how mindset in a specific discipline might invoke dramatically different responses to the same opportunity to learn.

I've seen Dweck's research misinterpreted to mean we can "repair" students' fixed mindsets by telling them we believe in them and they just need to keep trying. These are important messages for students to hear, but the response to that encouragement only matters if it better aligns their effort to relevant strategies. As we saw in the stand-up comedy non-exemplar, more effort applied to an ineffective strategy actually results in a diminished belief in ability. "Try harder" assumes the individual already has a complete skill set and deep understanding of the strategies necessary to improve.

To support a thriving response toward important goals for learning, responsive learners take a page from the expert's playbook; they "try differently" to better align effort to an effective strategy.

How do students' beliefs about others' abilities, strategies, and effort influence their responsiveness to opportunities to learn?

If you've ever seen a magician do a perfectly executed card trick, or seen a juggler toss five balls in the air and keep them moving as though they are floating, you've had that moment of awe where you ask yourself, "How can someone do that?" Though both acts elicit this amazed response, their approaches to their craft are completely different.

Figure 9.4

Fixed Mindset and the Coping Response Versus Growth Mindset and the Thriving Response

Fixed Mindset	Mindset and Response	Growth Mindset
"Good readers/writers/ scientists/mathematicians/ artists are born, not made."		"I can apply strategic efforts to learn new, challenging skills and understandings in this class."
Coping Response		**Thriving Response**
"This is too hard. I can't do it."	**Facing a Challenge**	"This is challenging, but I am going to struggle through until it starts to make sense."
"If I have to put forward a lot of effort, people will think I'm stupid. I'll play it off like I didn't try."	**Need for Effort**	"I will have to try hard to accomplish this. I'll need to be strategic."
"I've never seen a problem like this; I can't do it."	**Confronting the Unknown**	"This is new to me. I wonder if there are existing strategies I can apply?"
"I'm already good enough/ will never be good enough, so why bother?"	**Opportunity to Revise/Redo**	"This is an opportunity to learn from my mistakes and improve."
"Now my teacher knows I am bad at this too."	**Receiving Developmental Feedback**	"Feedback focuses my efforts to improve and improves the focus of my efforts."
"I'm not going to ask because I don't want anyone to think I'm dumb.	**Opportunities to Ask Questions**	"I ask questions to affirm what is working and inform my next efforts."
Strategic efforts to cope with being exposed as having limited ability to improve	**Result of Response**	**Strategic efforts to use strategies to improve skills and deepen understandings**

These examples are adapted from teachers' responses to the need to improve presented in Frontier & Mielke (p. 136, 2016).

Jugglers tell you exactly what they are going to do and then show you each step in the process. "Each of these five bowling balls weighs 14 pounds! Those of you in the front row may want to pay attention because I am going to juggle all of them at once!" The juggler may then throw one up in the air to show how heavy it is. He may begin by only juggling two to show how easy it is to get a finger stuck between them. Then he juggles three, then four, and then five. It's impressive because you can see—and appreciate—the fluency in the use of strategies to execute such a complex skill.

Unlike a juggler, magicians ask you to believe they have innate abilities that cannot be learned or explained. "Would you be amazed if I could tell you what your card is before you even picked it? I'm writing a card name on this piece of paper, and I'm setting it over here. Now I'd like you to pick a card, but don't show it to me." Magic is the process of fluently using strategies that are hidden from the audience. Magicians conceal their fluent use of strategies while distracting the audience with clutter (e.g., a wand, a flourish, an envelope, a handkerchief). By concealing their strategies, the audience is left thinking the only plausible explanation: "He must be magic!"

Too often, students see academic disciplines as magic. They falsely believe that ability, and not an appropriate application of strategies, determines one's success. Consider the following statements. Even though they are logically sound, the premise of each is deeply flawed:

> If magic is an innate skill, and I do not possess magical ability, then there is no point in me thinking about how magic works. I sit back, watch the gifted magician do things I can't explain, and marvel in disbelief. If magicians are born, and not made, the more I am in awe of a magician, the more I am convinced of my own inferiority. Rewatching someone else perform the same trick over and over and being told all you have to do is 'this, then this, then this' merely frustrates me. Being told I have to 'try harder' because this is really an important trick only proves that you think I have low ability because I should be able to do this already.

This student's response is based on debilitating, and widely held, misconceptions about learning. Go back and reread the statements but replace *magic* with *math, reading,* or *physics,* and replace *magician* with *teacher* or *high-achieving student.* This is the metacognitive voice of a learner on the path to learned helplessness. Our words and actions in the classroom can inadvertently affirm these misconceptions. As renowned graphic designer

Edward Tufte (1997) has noted, "The strategies of magic suggest what *not* to do" if our goal is to help people understand (p. 55).

Consider how the premise of each of these two metaphors—the magician and the juggler—results in behaviors that elicit dramatically different responses from observers (Figure 9.5). When we distract students with clutter and conceal strategies, they are more likely to attribute success or failure to special abilities and innate skills. When we explicitly model for students the effort and strategy involved in learning, the more likely they are to understand that anyone can improve their abilities by aligning strategy to effort. To support this thriving response, we need to intentionally direct students' attention to the strategies used to improve learning.

Figure 9.5

**Helping Students Prioritize Strategic Effort:
Teach Like a Juggler, not a Magician**

The Premise	Magicians rely on clutter to conceal strategy.	Jugglers rely on clarity to reveal strategy.
Focus	I create clutter that makes it difficult for you to see the transferrable strategies I am using.	I ask you to pay attention to exactly what I'll be doing. I will show you the transferrable strategies I am using.
Intentionality	I intentionally conceal strategies and never talk about what I am actually being metacognitive about.	I talk directly about what I am doing, what I will do next, why it is difficult, mishaps I've had along the way, and how I deal with the risks.
Purpose	My purpose is to impress you with my innate ability.	My purpose is to help you see how I've developed fluency in specific strategies that allow me to be responsive to challenge.
Observer's Response	"Wow! I'm not a magician; there's no way I could do that!"	"Wow! With some focus, practice, and strategy, I could juggle too!"

How do effective teachers protect and develop each student's ability to prioritize strategic efforts to learn?

The etymology of the word *curriculum* is a pathway, and *standard* is a flag that marks rallying points along a path. Given the origins of these words, consider two anecdotes as metaphors for how we guide our students through a curriculum to achieve standards.

Have you ever gone on a walking tour in a city you were visiting? Typically, it goes something like this. A deeply knowledgeable guide leads a group along a predetermined path of specific landmarks. The guide talks about a landmark and then asks if there are any questions. To protect anyone from getting lost, the guide keeps everyone together. To ensure the group stays on schedule, the guide reminds those who fall behind to hurry along. After seeing seven or eight landmarks, the tour is over and you and your guide part ways.

As a metaphor for classroom teaching, a walking tour from a knowledgeable guide represents an efficient strategy to transmit surface-level knowledge. Time is limited, and we accept the cursory but efficient method of showing and telling. The tour guide puts forth most of the effort and does all the talking, and the tourists passively receive information. "We don't have much time, but I'll show you as much as I can, and I'll tell you as many details as possible about what I think is most important."

This is an efficient approach to deliver information to a group of passive recipients, but it is not a very effective strategy to support deep learning. What happens if this is the dominant mode of instruction?

In their book *The Teaching Gap* (1999), James Stigler and James Hiebert compared and contrasted instructional methods in U.S., German, and Japanese schools to better understand why German and Japanese students performed at higher levels on international assessments. They found that U.S. classrooms tended to rely on teacher-centered, coverage-based instructional strategies where teachers put forth most of the effort to tell students about terms and demonstrate procedures. Students focused their efforts on learning new content each day.

By contrast, the German and Japanese teachers were four times more likely to spend time developing students' understanding of important concepts by engaging them in strategies that required guided inquiry, feedback, revision, and application. Less content was covered in these classrooms, but students were given opportunities to engage in the strategic effort to make meaning at a deeper level. Although a "stroll and show" approach is an efficient strategy to expose students to surface-level knowledge, it does not allow students the time to focus their efforts on learning that will result in deep understanding. Teaching for depth requires an entirely different metaphor.

Anyone who has ever climbed to the summit of Mount Everest has done so with the assistance of a Sherpa mountain guide. The Sherpa people are a Nepalese ethnic group who live in and near the Himalayan mountain range. Over thousands of years, they have acclimated to live comfortably at elevations of 5,000 meters. This is remarkable because hypoxia, the human body's fatal response to thin air at high altitude, begins at an elevation of about 3,000 meters. Base camp on the Nepalese side of Mount Everest is at an elevation greater than 5,300 meters. Everest's peak is at the cruising altitude of a commercial jet: 8,848 meters, or just a shade over 29,000 feet.

A good mountain guide knows that if you want to reach the peak, you need to follow an intentional, strategic, 60-day process designed to help you slowly acclimate to the increasingly challenging conditions before you push to the summit. When you arrive at base camp, you can see the peak of the mountain, but seeing the goal and engaging in the strategic effort to be able to actually reach that goal are very different things. If you want to actually make it to the summit—and return safely—the guide must protect and develop your ability to prioritize your strategy and effort.

Although the path to the summit is linear, the strategic route is recursive and circuitous. If you were to attempt to go up the mountain in an efficient, linear path, you would not survive. Therefore, the guide uses expertise to protect your instincts from moving too quickly. The guide charts a strategic route by which you incrementally climb up and down increasingly challenging portions of the mountain so you can acclimate to the higher altitudes. As you get closer to the summit, the goal is easier to see but harder to attain. The dangers of frostbite and hypoxia are very real. The strategy and effort required to achieve success on the final portions of the climb are dramatically different than those that were used during earlier stages. By this point, a good mountain guide should have developed your capacity to be successful in these final stages and will help you align your use of strategies to the focused effort required to achieve the goal—to reach the summit and return safely.

Traversing a mountain is a much richer metaphor for the complexity of protecting and developing a student's capacity to attain rigorous learning goals. The effective, efficient strategies for teaching and attaining surface level-goals are different than those required for teaching and attaining deep understanding. The teacher and the learner must utilize different strategies to navigate the circuitous path that leads to deep understanding. As Marzano (2009) reminds us, a "specific instructional strategy is effective only when it is used in the specific situation for which it was designed" (p. 34).

In a responsive learning environment, teachers protect and develop students' ability to prioritize their strategic efforts to learn. Likewise, responsive learners prioritize their efforts and apply strategies to achieve a goal (Figure 9.6).

Responsive Learning: Action Steps

Responsive learners are able to prioritize their strategy and effort to develop important skills and understandings. To minimize clutter and create clarity to support conditions for responsive learning, use the following action steps.

- Develop students' ability to strategize by aligning strategies and tasks to learning goals and success criteria.
- Develop students' ability to plan, monitor, and evaluate the relationship among effort, strategy, and results.
- Protect students' ability to prioritize.

Action Step 1

Develop students' ability to strategize by aligning strategies and tasks to learning goals and success criteria. Responsive teachers prioritize their students' strategic efforts to learn, and responsive learners believe they can accomplish a task through strategic effort. So far, we've engaged in a process to create clarity by establishing a shared purpose and priorities at the system, discipline, course, and unit levels. These elements create a continuous, recursive thread that connects what it means to understand with what is most important to understand. Now it's time to turn that potential into action at the point of contact between the teacher and learner by aligning instructional strategies to prioritized learning goals and shared success criteria.

Figure 9.6

Alignment of Shared Success Criteria, Learning Goals, and Instructional Strategies

	Unistructural	Multistructural	Relational	Extended Abstract
If learning goals are aligned to...	The student is able to • tell • memorize (in isolation) • identify (isolated parts) • define (basic) • recall • follow rote steps • apply simple formulas • give (basic)	The student is able to • tell more • memorize (and apply) • identify (characteristics) • define (complex terms) • give (complex examples) • describe • organize and classify • apply a series of steps	The student is able to • compare and contrast • explain/connect • argue, given claim/evidence • analyze, given framework • apply to similar contexts • translate and apply • interpret meaning • perform fluently	On open-ended, authentic tasks, the student is able to • design/create and justify/explain • determine and justify • hypothesize and justify/explain • generate criteria and analyze • generate criteria and strategize • generate claim and support • evaluate and explain • interpret and perform fluently
Then examples of aligned instructional strategies include	• Overt connections to existing schema • Compare and contrast to existing schema • Vocabulary attainment/Basic Frayer Model • Sorting • Error identification, summary statements • Process diagrams/graphic organizers • Memory strategies; mnemonics • Two- and three-column charts • Sorting • Massed and distributed practice		• Error analysis, correction, explanation • Examine similarities and differences • Classify and justify • Complex Frayer Model • Generate flowcharts • Support given claims • Explain processes • Concept attainment • Graphic organizers with summary statements	• Experimental inquiry • Problem-solving tasks with process or product constraints • Decision-making tasks based on justification using specific criteria • Historical, definitional, projective, or counterfactual investigation tasks • Authentic performance tasks (role, audience, format, topic)

For detailed discussion on aligning research-based instructional strategies to specific types of learning goals, see Marzano, 2007; Marzano, 2017; and McTighe & Silver, 2020.

Expert teachers use the right instructional strategy, in the right way, at the right time, to prioritize students' strategic effort to learn. Students are more responsive to opportunities to learn when they believe they have the capacity to achieve a specific goal by aligning strategy to effort. To support this thriving response, think like a mountain guide. Explicitly show students how strategies can be applied to focus their efforts to use the right strategy, in the right way, and at the right time, depending on where one is on the circuitous path toward a challenging goal.

To support our students' willingness and capacity to be responsive to opportunities to learn, we need to ensure they are clear about the relationship between the goal they are pursuing and where to invest effort in a strategy to improve. Figure 9.7 shows how specific instructional strategies can be used to focus students' use of strategies that are aligned to the specific types of acquisition, organization, elaboration, and synthesis articulated in the learning goals for a specific academic context.

Note how the transferable strategies form a bridge that prioritizes students' effort to engage in an activity that will ultimately help them attain each learning goal as aligned to the priority standard area:

- Vocabulary acquisition and massed practice are strategies aligned to the learning goals related to *defining terms* and *rote learning.*
- Organizing terms and writing summary statements are strategies aligned to the learning goals related to *describing specific attributes of multiple parts of a system.*
- Generating flowcharts and synthesis statements are strategies aligned to learning goals related to *making connections* and *describing relationships.*
- Developing and justifying an extended metaphor is a strategy aligned to the learning goal of *transferring understanding to a new context.*

By the end of the unit, students will be able to explain the form and function of the periodic table at the extended abstract level. This is not a passive "walking tour" past the elements; it is recursive climb up (and down) a mountain to adapt to unique, and increasingly complex, conditions. The tasks and prompts at the more complex levels are hands-on and engaging.

Figure 9.7

Alignment of a Priority Standard to a Standard-Specific Learning Goal and Strategies/Activities

	Unistructural	Multistructural	Relational	Extended Abstract
Success Criteria Aligned to Priority Standard *"Constructs Written Explanations"*	Identifies or defines important facts and relevant examples as related to a science topic.	Describes scientific objects, processes, phenomenon, or models stating important facts and relevant details and examples.	Explains a scientific object, process, model, or phenomenon accurately by identifying and describing important relationships among scientific ideas, concepts, and facts, using precise vocabulary and relevant examples.	Develops coherent explanations about a scientific object, process, model, or phenomenon by explaining important relationships and distinctions among scientific ideas, concepts, and facts, using precise vocabulary and well-chosen examples.
Aligned Learning Goals for a Science Unit on the Periodic Table	I can define *atom, proton, nucleus, atomic number, chemical symbol, element name, atomic weight, group,* and *period.*	I can describe "the rules" of how the periodic table is organized, based on atomic number, physical properties, chemical properties, groups, and periods.	I can explain the form and function of how the periodic table of elements is used to organize atomic matter, based on physical and chemical patterns and relationships within and between atoms.	I can transfer my understanding of the periodic table to explain important patterns, relationships, and distinctions among elements of matter based on their physical and chemical properties. (using precise science vocabulary).
Examples of Aligned Strategies	• Vocabulary acquisition • Massed practice	• Organize terms based on essential attributes • Summary statements	• Generate flow charts to explain processes • Academic games	• Generate, explain, and critique extended metaphors

	Unistructural	Multistructural	Relational	Extended Abstract
Examples of Aligned Activities	• Complete the five-step vocabulary acquisition framework template for atom, atomic number, and group. • Create vocabulary notecards for priority vocabulary and review terms to build understanding.	• Complete the Term, Structure, Function three-column chart for the terms *group* and *period*. Use *atomic number*, *physical properties*, and *chemical properties* in each response. • Write summary statements for *group* and *period*.	Write eight yes/no questions you can ask to identify the correct element every time. Then explain how your questions work as related to the structure and function of the periodic table.	Create a "wanted poster" for an element. Include a sketch, what it is wanted for, and a brief written description of known associates, typical hangouts, size and weight, appearance at room temperature and in extreme heat, whether it is dangerous, and if so, under what conditions.

Just as important, they give students the opportunity to apply strategies—organizing flowcharts, asking relevant questions, and developing extended metaphors—that will develop their depth and sophistication of understanding and allow them to generate evidence of understanding at the extended abstract level of the success criteria.

Action Step 2

Develop students' ability to plan, monitor, and evaluate the relationship among effort, strategy, and results. In Chapter 6, we talked about the importance of gathering metacognitive evidence to make each student's internal voice of strategic reasoning visible. These questions can be as simple as "Explain your reasoning" or "Explain how you . . ." This type of evidence allows us to make inferences about students' depth and intentionality (described as tacit, aware, strategic, or reflective) in applying strategies to complete an assessment task.

Now we turn our attention to developing students' ability to navigate three phases of metacognition that are used to plan, monitor, and evaluate the effectiveness of their strategic efforts to learn. Building a responsive metacognitive voice has been shown to empower students to take control of their own learning, improve their academic achievement, and help them transfer learning to new contexts (Cambridge International Teaching and Learning Team, 2019).

Planning to learn involves awareness of the relationships among current skills and understandings as related to learning goals and success criteria. The following are examples of questions and tasks that can be used to give students the opportunity to plan productive responses to learning:

Planning to achieve learning goals and success criteria

- Restate the learning goal/success criteria in your own words.
- What do you already know about this content/concept/skill?
- Restate the purpose of the assignment/task/project in your own words.
- Underline the parts of the assignment/task/project/success criteria that are clear to you.
- Circle the parts of the assignment/task/project/success criteria that are unclear to you.

Planning for strategic effort

- What are the steps you'll need to take to solve/complete this assignment/task/project?
- What information required to solve/complete this assignment/task/prompt is known? What is unknown?
- What do you already know that will help you solve/complete this assignment/task/prompt?
- Describe a strategy you will use to achieve the goal/accomplish the task.
- What will you do if you get stuck?

Monitoring strategy and effort involves awareness—in real time—of the efficiency and effectiveness of strategies to produce high-quality work as aligned to success criteria. Efficiency is about the amount of effort put forth to make progress on a task. Effectiveness is about the usefulness of a particular strategy to accomplish a task. The following are examples of questions that can be used to help students monitor the effectiveness of their strategy and effort:

Monitoring progress toward accomplishing a task and demonstrating evidence of success criteria

- What is going well on this assignment/project? Why?
- What content/concept/skill is becoming clearer to you? What have you done to make that possible?
- What content/concept/skill is confusing to you?

Monitoring effectiveness of strategic effort

- What strategies are working well and why?
- Where are you getting stuck and why?
- If you are stuck, how might you apply the same strategy differently? How might this help?
- If you are stuck, what is a different strategy you can try? How might this help?

Evaluating results involves a summative self-assessment or self-reflection. Self-assessment allows the learner to describe how evidence of learning relates to success criteria, whereas self-reflection allows the learner to reflect on the effectiveness of strategies used to improve. The following are examples of sentence frames, questions, and tasks that can be used to give students the opportunity to self-assess and self-reflect:

Self-assessment of the quality of my work (evaluation of evidence related to success criteria)

- The best part of my work is . . . because . . .
- Explain why you chose to . . .

Using the language of the success criteria, I think someone looking at my work would say . . .

- Something that is now clearer as a result of doing this assignment/task/project is . . .
- How does this work show (a specific element of the success criteria)? What did you do, specifically, to accomplish that?

Self-reflection about the process (evaluation of the effectiveness of strategy and effort)

- A strategy or approach that worked well and I should continue to do is . . .
- Describe a specific choice you made, or an action you took, that you think contributed to the quality of this assignment/task/project as related to the success criteria.
- What's something the teacher could have done that would have made the assignment/task/prompt/success criteria clearer to you?

These questions are very different than those that are typically asked of students, which is precisely what makes them so powerful. Be selective when asking for students' responses to these types of questions, and then ask those questions frequently. Asking one or two of these questions every few months is no more productive than an occasional trip to the gym. The goal is to prioritize your students' efforts to focus on a few of these questions until they become habits of mind. The time you invest will pay dividends as students learn to develop and honor the internal voice that can support a thriving response to learning.

Action Step 3

Protect students' ability to prioritize. Consider the dichotomies for clutter and clarity in Figure 9.8. If you were to ask graduating high school seniors which column best describes their schooling experience, which do you think they'd select? The clutter column requires more effort and energy to attain fewer results. Because teachers' collective energy and efforts are misaligned, they will always lack the clarity

Figure 9.8

Clutter or Clarity?

Systems That Create Clutter	Systems That Create Clarity
Scattered: High effort yields few results because expectations for quality change from task to task, unit to unit, course to course, and teacher to teacher.	Focused: Prioritization of shared success criteria as aligned to the most important standards; evidence of understanding is described at a systems level.
Random: High effort and lack of clarity as to what assessment evidence is most important or what results mean.	Intentional: Assessment is used to align efforts toward the most important evidence as aligned to the most important success criteria.
Arbitrary: Expectations for quality, and judgments about the quality of work and students' progress, are seen as subjective and arbitrary.	Reliable: Consistent, accurate inferences about learners' progress are based on shared meaning of the most important evidence and success criteria.
Transactional: Feedback is given to students to record points, justify grades, or hold them accountable.	Meaningful: Shared understanding of how evidence relates to success criteria is used to provide meaningful feedback; because students see the feedback as meaningful, they use it to improve.
Effortful: Teachers and students spend a lot of time sifting through textbooks, the internet, and instructional resources to cover content and complete tasks.	Purposeful: Curriculum, instruction, and assessment are intentionally aligned to prioritize students' efforts related to what is most important to learn.
Reactive: The assumption is that the system has achieved maximal efficiency. If a student is struggling, it is due to a deficiency in the child that must be fixed.	Responsive: Responsive teachers prioritize their students' strategic efforts to learn. Responsive learners believe they can accomplish a task through strategic effort.

and focus required to help students prioritize their own efforts to learn. The system has chosen clutter.

Conversely, the "clarity" column is what happens when individuals within a system prioritize and align their efforts around the most important standards and shared success criteria. By adopting a few nonnegotiable constraints, less effort can be applied with greater focus to help students improve in the areas that matter most. Clarity doesn't happen by chance. Clarity happens by choice.

The first step to solving a problem is acknowledging that one exists. If we are serious about protecting our students' ability to prioritize, we need to acknowledge the root causes of clutter and look for evidence of how clutter and the clarity paradox impede the effectiveness of our teaching and can have a debilitating impact on learners and learning. As you read the descriptors in Figure 9.9, take an empathetic approach. Stand in your students' shoes and ask yourself if they notice evidence of clutter or the clarity paradox. They might not have the vocabulary or insight to explain what they experience in the language we've used throughout this book, but the results are predictable: they internalize their inability to navigate clutter as an internal deficiency in their ability to learn.

Figure 9.9

Systems That Choose Clutter: Indicators of Concern

Causes of Clutter	Evidence of Clutter	Evidence of the Clarity Paradox
Scattered Priorities for Learning	• Little or no articulation of what is important in a discipline or course. • Little or no articulation of what it means to understand in a discipline or course. • Success criteria are arbitrary. • Students and teachers are overwhelmed with expectations and resources.	Individual teachers establish their own priorities for curricular programs, use their own descriptors and scales for success criteria, and use their own definitions of key assessment terms—but students see clutter as they move from course to course and grade to grade.
Random Assessment	• Assessment tasks are not aligned to priority standards or shared success criteria. • Tasks emphasize coverage of a lot of surface-level knowledge or activities detached from standards.	Assessments are aligned to teacher's own expectations or interests—but students see little or no continuity related to the most important evidence of learning as they move from course to course or grade to grade.
Arbitrary Expectations	• Individual tasks are assessed with different success criteria each time. • Success criteria are based on what is easy to observe (e.g., directions, quantitative descriptors) rather than important evidence of understanding.	Individual teachers can justify their expectations for how assessment evidence relates to their own success criteria—but as students move from teacher to teacher, they see expectations as arbitrary.

Transactional Feedback	• Feedback is justification of a grade, about effort rather than strategy, about the task rather than the standards, or given as vague praise. • There is little or no expectation that students are to use feedback in meaningful ways to improve.	Individual teachers can justify the validity of their feedback and give thoughtful feedback to students—but students don't know how feedback "works" and aren't sure what to do with it.
Effortful Teaching	• The curriculum invests a lot of time in activities without understanding or in coverage of content without prioritized constraints. • Everything is taught, and everything is of equal importance. • Teachers put forth tremendous effort but are frustrated with results. • Students prioritize efforts to comply or forget, rather than learn.	Individual teachers can justify their curriculum and assessment, but as students take different courses, there is little continuity among standards, success criteria, and priorities. Teachers believe they have to put forth a lot of effort to catch students up or reteach what they believe should have been taught.
Reactive Learning	• Students are overwhelmed with expectations amidst a misalignment of expectation and opportunity resulting in a disconnect among ability, effort, and strategy, resulting in a diminished belief in one's capacity to learn. • If students don't do well, it is assumed to be due to a deficiency in the student.	Due to a lack of continuity across programs and courses, students don't have time to develop the most important transferable skills and strategies. Alternatively, teachers don't see their discipline from the perspective of a novice and fail to provide important opportunities to learn.

Fortunately, once evidence of the clutter problem and the clarity paradox has been identified, we can do something about it. The action steps described throughout this book can be used as a road map toward system-level clarity. Figure 9.10 shows success criteria (for us, not our students!) that would be evident in a system that has prioritized and aligned teachers' and students' strategic efforts to learn.

Throughout this book, we've articulated a systemic approach to prioritizing collective efforts aligned to what is most important to learn and what it means to learn. This approach requires the disciplined use of a framework that makes it possible to choose clarity through prioritized constraints. These constraints reap the greatest benefits for teaching and learning when they are used by everyone in the system to guide choices about what they will—and will not—do. Prioritizing without decluttering is really just reorganizing the clutter. If we are going to protect our students' ability to prioritize their

Figure 9.10

Systems That Choose Clarity: Evidence of Success

Shared Priorities	Evidence of System-Level Clarity for Teachers and Teaching	Evidence of System-Level Clarity for Learners and Learning
Focused Success Criteria	We use a shared scale for success criteria as aligned to a manageable number of prioritized standards to focus our collective attention and energy on what is most important to learn and what it means to learn.	Students see clear, consistent expectations for what it means to understand and clear priorities for what is most important to understand across programs, courses, units, and lessons.
Intentional Assessment	We use a shared language of assessment terms and are intentional in designing high-quality assessment tasks to gather the most important evidence of learning as aligned to the prioritized standards and success criteria.	Students can prioritize their attention and strategic effort to focus on assessment tasks that are intentionally designed to minimize clutter and elicit clear evidence of important understandings.
Reliable Inferences	We agree how the most important assessment evidence relates to the most relevant level of shared success criteria. We have established a high level of interrater reliability in evaluating students' work.	Students have a clear and accurate understanding of how success criteria can be used to describe their assessment evidence, and they use that information to plan, monitor, and evaluate their strategic efforts to learn.
Meaningful Feedback	We use our shared understanding of how assessment evidence relates to success criteria to give high-quality judgmental and developmental feedback that is used by students in meaningful ways to prioritize their strategic efforts to learn.	Students are clear about the purpose of judgmental and developmental feedback and use feedback in meaningful ways to affirm and inform their strategic efforts to learn.
Shared Purpose	We establish a shared purpose for learning and communicate a clear, concise, and consistent set of priorities related to what it most important to understand and what it means to understand across programs, courses, units, and lessons.	Students are clear about the purpose of school, courses, units, and lessons. They prioritize their strategic efforts to deepen and internalize their understanding of what is most important to learn, and they transfer those understandings to authentic contexts.
Responsive Teaching and Learning	We protect students' ability to prioritize and develop their capacity to invest effort in the deliberate use of strategies that empower them to be responsive to opportunities to learn.	Students believe strategic effort is more important than innate ability and trust their teachers to provide learning opportunities that help them prioritize their strategic efforts to learn.

strategic efforts to learn, we need to commit to using resources and making decisions each day that are focused, intentional, reliable, meaningful, and purposeful to ensure the system is responsive to their learning needs.

For a summary of important ideas and strategies discussed in this chapter, see Figure 9.11.

Responsive Learning: Revisiting the Scenarios

In the first scenario (The unresponsive path to learned helplessness), despite the concern and care demonstrated by the teacher, the conditions for responsive learning were not present. This course was a walking tour past some interesting landmarks. It emphasized coverage of content rather than using specific instructional strategies designed to scaffold students to deeper levels of understanding. Furthermore, the course concealed how comedians use strategies to *think like a comedian*. Because of the absence of reliable success criteria and valid assessment evidence, the teacher was not able to make reliable inferences about where students should prioritize strategic efforts to learn. The feedback given to the student to improve was invalid. When the student responded to the feedback and still did poorly, he attributed his inability to demonstrate evidence of understanding as an internal deficiency rather than as an inability to develop and apply appropriate strategies.

In the second scenario (How alignment supports a thriving response), the teacher revised the course to effectively align elements to prioritize her students' strategic efforts to learn. There is a clear focus on important priority standards that have been aligned to a reliable scale for success criteria. The revised assessment tasks intentionally direct students' attention and effort to the most important content, skills, and strategies throughout the entire course. Because the evidence is a valid representation of what is most important, the teacher—and her students—are able to make accurate, reliable inferences and generate meaningful feedback to affirm and inform next efforts for learning. The purpose of the course is now clear. Students are well positioned to be responsive to the opportunities that are presented throughout the course to prioritize their strategic efforts to learn.

Responsive Learning: Questions for Discussion and Reflection

- How do I/we clarify for students that aligning strategies and effort to learning goals is more important than innate ability?
- How do I/we use the right instructional strategy, in the right way, at the right time to support students to prioritize their strategic effort to learn?
- If components described in this chapter were implemented in our school/district, how might teachers and students benefit after a few years of consistent efforts to use them to prioritize students' strategic efforts to learn?

Figure 9.11
_____

Responsive Learning: Avoiding Clutter, Minimizing the Clarity Paradox, and Choosing Clarity

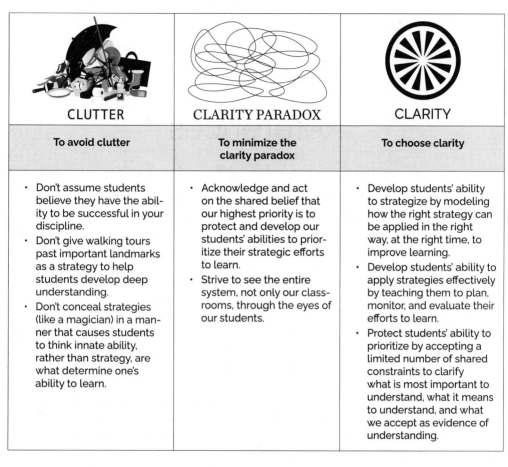

CLUTTER	CLARITY PARADOX	CLARITY
To avoid clutter	**To minimize the clarity paradox**	**To choose clarity**
• Don't assume students believe they have the ability to be successful in your discipline. • Don't give walking tours past important landmarks as a strategy to help students develop deep understanding. • Don't conceal strategies (like a magician) in a manner that causes students to think innate ability, rather than strategy, are what determine one's ability to learn.	• Acknowledge and act on the shared belief that our highest priority is to protect and develop our students' abilities to prioritize their strategic efforts to learn. • Strive to see the entire system, not only our classrooms, through the eyes of our students.	• Develop students' ability to strategize by modeling how the right strategy can be applied in the right way, at the right time, to improve learning. • Develop students' ability to apply strategies effectively by teaching them to plan, monitor, and evaluate their efforts to learn. • Protect students' ability to prioritize by accepting a limited number of shared constraints to clarify what is most important to understand, what it means to understand, and what we accept as evidence of understanding.

References

Anderson, L. W., & Krathwohl, D. R. (2001). *A taxonomy for learning, teaching, and assessing: A revision of Bloom's Taxonomy of educational objectives*. New York: Longman.

Apgar, V. (1953). A proposal for a new method of evaluation of the newborn infant. *Current Researches in Anesthesia & Analgesia, 32*(4), 260–267.

Barrett, F. J. (2012). *Yes to the mess: Surprising leadership lessons from jazz*. Brighton, MA: Harvard Business Review.

Biggs, J., & Tang, C. (2011). *Teaching for quality learning at university*. Maidenhead, UK: Open University Press.

Biggs, J. B., & Collis, K. F. (1982). *Evaluating the quality of learning: The SOLO taxonomy (structure of the observed learning outcome)*. New York: Academic Press.

Brookhart, S. (2017). *How to give effective feedback to your students, 2nd ed.* Alexandria, VA: ASCD.

Bruner, J. (1960). *The process of education*. Cambridge, MA: Harvard University Press.

Cambridge International Teaching and Learning Team. (2019). *Getting started with metacognition*. Retrieved from https://cambridge-community.org.uk/professional-development/gswmeta/index.html

Cohen, S. A. (1987). Instructional alignment: Searching for a magic bullet. *Educational Researcher, 16*(8), 16–20.

Dweck, C. S. (2000). *Self-theories: Their role in motivation, personality, and development*. Philadelphia: Psychology Press.

Dweck, C.S. (2006). *Mindset: The new psychology of success*. New York: Random House.

Dweck, C. S. (2007). The perils and promises of praise. *Educational Leadership, 65*(2), 34–39.

Dweck, C. S. (2010). Mind-sets and equitable education. *Principal Leadership, 10*(5), 26–29.

Ericsson, K. A. (2006). The influence of experience and deliberate practice on the development of superior expert performance. In K. A. Ericsson, N. Charness, P. Feltovichm, & R. R. Hoffman (Eds.), *Cambridge handbook of expertise and expert performance* (pp. 685–706). Cambridge, UK: Cambridge University Press.

Ericsson, K. A., Krampe, R. T., & Tesch-Romer, C. (1993). The role of deliberate practice in the acquisition of expert performance. *Psychological Review, 100*(3), 363-406.

Ericsson, K. A., & Pool, R. (2016). *Peak: Secrets from the new science of expertise.* Boston: Mariner Books.

Finster, M., & Wood, M. (2005). The Apgar score has survived the test of time. Anesthesiology, 102(4): 855–857.

Flavell, J. H. (1979). Metacognitions and cognitive monitoring: A new area of cognitive-developmental inquiry. *American Psychologist, 34,* 906–911.

Frontier, T., & Mielke, P. (2016). *Making teachers better, not bitter: Balancing evaluation, supervision, and reflection for professional growth.* Alexandria, VA: ASCD.

Frontier, T., & Rickabaugh, J. (2014). *Five levers to improve learning: How to prioritize for powerful results in your school.* Alexandria, VA: ASCD.

Gallup. (2016). 2016 Gallup student poll: A snapshot of results and findings. Retrieved from www.gallup.com

Gardner, H. (2000). *The disciplined mind: Beyond facts and standardized tests, the K–12 education that every child deserves.* New York: Penguin.

Gawande, A. (2007). *Better: A surgeon's notes on performance.* New York: Metropolitan Books.

Guskey, T. R., & Brookhart, S. M. (2019). *What we know about grading: What works, what doesn't, and what's next.* Alexandria, VA: ASCD.

Hattie, J. (2009). *Visible Learning: A synthesis of over 800 meta-analyses relating to achievement.* New York: Routledge.

Hattie, J. (2012). *Visible learning for teachers: Maximizing impact on learning.* New York: Routledge.

Hattie, J., & Timperley, H. (2007). The power of feedback. *Review of Educational Research, 77*(1), 81–112.

Hyland, F., & Hyland, K. (2001). Sugaring the pill. Praise and criticism in written feedback. *Journal of Second Language Writing, 10*(3), 185–212.

Kelley, T., & Kelley, D. (2013). *Creative confidence: Unleashing the creative potential within us all.* New York: Crown Publishing Group.

Kondo, M. (2014). *The life-changing magic of tidying up: The Japanese art of decluttering and organizing.* Berkeley: Ten Speed Press.

Maier, S. F., & Seligman M. E. (2016). Learned helplessness at fifty: Insights from neuroscience. *Psychological Review, 123*(4), 349–367.

Marzano, R. J. (2007). *The art and science of teaching: A comprehensive framework for effective instruction.* Alexandria, VA: ASCD.

Marzano, R. J. (2009). Setting the record straight on "high-yield" strategies. *Phi Delta Kappan, 91*(1), 30–37.

Marzano, R. J. (2017). *The new art and science of teaching.* Alexandria, VA: ASCD.

McKeown, G. (2014). *Essentialism: The disciplined pursuit of less.* New York: Crown Business.

McTighe, J. (2014). Long-term transfer goals. Retrieved from https://jaymctighe.com/downloads/Long-term-Transfer-Goals.pdf

McTighe, J., & Silver, H. F. (2020). *Teaching for deeper learning: Tools to engage students in meaning making.* Alexandria, VA: ASCD.

Moss, C. M., & Brookhart, S. M. (2012). *Learning targets: Helping students aim for understanding in today's lesson.* Alexandria, VA: ASCD.

New South Wales Department of Education. (2017). *Cognitive load theory: Research that teachers really need to understand.* Sydney, Australia: Centre for Education Statistics and Evaluation.

Perkins, D. (1992). *Smart schools: Better thinking and learning for every child.* New York: Free Press.

Perkins, D. (2009). *Making learning whole.* San Francisco: Jossey-Bass.

Pinker, S. (2014). *The sense of style.* New York: Viking.

Pope, D. C. (2001). *Doing school: How we are creating a generation of stressed out, materialistic, and miseducated students.* New Haven, CT: Yale University Press.

Popham, J. (2010). *Everything school leaders need to know about assessment.* Thousand Oaks, CA: Corwin Press.

Seligman, M. E., & Maier, S. F. (1967). Failure to escape traumatic shock. *Journal of Experimental Psychology, 74*(1), 1–9.

Simon, H. A. (1971) Designing organizations for an information-rich world. In *Computers, communications, and the public interest* (pp. 38–72), M. Greenberger, Ed. Baltimore, MD: The Johns Hopkins Press.

Statista. (2021). Life expectancy (from birth) in the United States, from 1860 to 2020. Retrieved from www.statista.com/statistics/1040079/life-expectancy-united-states-all-time

Stiggins, R. J. (2001). *Student-involved classroom assessment* (3rd ed.). Upper Saddle River, NJ: Prentice Hall.

Stiggins, R. J. (2007). Assessment through the student's eyes. *Educational Leadership, 64*(8), 22–26.

Stigler, J. W., & Hiebert, J. (1999). *The teaching gap: Best ideas from the world's teachers for improving education in the classroom.* New York: The Free Press.

Stone, D., & Heen, S. (2014). *Thanks for the feedback: The science and art of receiving feedback well.* New York: Penguin.

Sweller, J. (2016). Working memory, long-term memory, and instructional design. *Journal of Applied Research in Memory and Cognition, 5*(4), 360–367.

Tatsumi, N. (2005). *The art of discarding: How to get rid of clutter and find joy.* New York: Hachette.

Tufte, E. R. (1997). *Visual explanations: Images and quantities, evidence and narrative.* Cheshire, CT: Graphics Press.

Tyler, S. (2001). *The perfect teaching tool?* Paper presented to Learning Matters Symposium. Melbourne: Victoria University.

Webb, N. (1997). *Criteria for alignment of expectations and assessments in mathematics and science education. Research Monograph No. 6.* Madison, WI: University of Wisconsin-Madison National Center for Improving Science Education.

Wiggins, G., & McTighe, J. (2005). *Understanding by design* (Expanded 2nd ed.). Alexandria, VA: ASCD.

Wiliam, D. (2016). The secret of effective feedback. *Educational Leadership, 73*(7), 10–15.

Wu, T. (2016). *The attention merchants: The epic scramble to get inside our heads.* New York: Knopf.

Index

The letter *f* following a page locator denotes a figure.

About the Author

 **Tony Frontier**, PhD, is an award-winning educator who works with teachers and school leaders nationally and internationally to help them prioritize efforts to improve student learning. With expertise in student engagement, evidence-based assessment, effective instruction, teacher reflection, data analysis, and strategic planning, Frontier emphasizes a systems approach to build capacity and empower teachers to improve each student's schooling experience.

Frontier is coauthor of the ASCD books *Five Levers to Improve Learning: How to Prioritize for Powerful Results in Your School* with James Rickabaugh; *Effective Supervision: Supporting the Art and Science of Teaching* with Robert J. Marzano and David Livingston; and *Making Teachers Better, Not Bitter: Balancing Evaluation, Supervision, and Reflection for Professional Growth* with Paul Mielke. He is also coauthor of *Creating Passionate Learners: Engaging Today's Students for Tomorrow's World* with Kim Brown and Donald J. Viegut (Corwin). Frontier is a frequent contributor to ASCD's *Educational Leadership,* and his books have been translated and published in Korean, Mandarin, and Arabic.

In addition to his work as an author and a consultant, Frontier serves as an associate professor of doctoral leadership studies at Cardinal Stritch University in Milwaukee, Wisconsin, where he teaches courses in curriculum development, organizational learning, research methods, and statistics.

As a former classroom teacher in Milwaukee Public Schools, an associate high school principal, and the director of curriculum and instruction for the Whitefish Bay School District, Frontier brings a wealth of experience as a classroom teacher, building administrator, and central office administrator to his workshops, writing, and research. As a professional musician and photographer, he is always listening and looking for metaphors in the arts and humanities to challenge old assumptions or to support new ways of thinking about the many challenges and opportunities faced each day by teachers and learners.

He can be reached at tonyfrontier@gmail.com and on Twitter at @tonyfrontier.

Related ASCD Resources: Teaching

At the time of publication, the following resources were available (ASCD stock numbers in parentheses).

Advancing Formative Assessment in Every Classroom: A Guide for Instructional Leaders, 2nd Ed. by Connie M. Moss & Susan M. Brookhart (#120005)

Designing Authentic Performance Tasks and Projects: Tools for Meaningful Learning and Assessment by Jay McTighe, Kristina J. Doubet & Eric M. Carbaugh (#119021)

Five Levers to Improve Learning: How to Prioritize for Powerful Results in Your School by Tony Frontier & James Rickabaugh (#114002)

Focus: Elevating the Essentials to Radically Improve Student Learning, 2nd Ed. by Mike Schmoker (#118044)

How to Give Effective Feedback to Your Students, 2nd Ed. by Susan M. Brookhart (#116066)

How to Look at Student Work to Uncover Student Thinking by Susan M. Brookhart & Alice Oakley (#122011)

Leading with Focus: Elevating the Essentials for School and District Improvement by Mike Schmoker (#116024)

Making Curriculum Matter: How to Build SEL, Equity, and Other Priorities into Daily Instruction by Angela Di Michele Lalor (#122007)

Making Teachers Better, Not Bitter: Balancing Evaluation, Supervision, and Reflection for Professional Growth by Tony Frontier & Paul Mielke (#116002)

The Minimalist Teacher by Tamera Musiowsky-Borneman & C. Y. Arnold (#121058)

For up-to-date information about ASCD resources, go to www.ascd.org. You can search the complete archives of *Educational Leadership* at www.ascd.org/el.

ASCD myTeachSource®
Download resources from a professional learning platform with hundreds of research-based best practices and tools for your classroom at http://myteach-source.ascd.org/

For more information, send an email to member@ascd.org; call 1-800-933-2723 or 703-578-9600; send a fax to 703-575-5400; or write to Information Services, ASCD, 1703 N. Beauregard St., Alexandria, VA 22311-1714 USA.

WHOLE CHILD
TENETS

1 HEALTHY
Each student enters school healthy and learns about and practices a healthy lifestyle.

2 SAFE
Each student learns in an environment that is physically and emotionally safe for students and adults.

3 ENGAGED
Each student is actively engaged in learning and is connected to the school and broader community.

4 SUPPORTED
Each student has access to personalized learning and is supported by qualified, caring adults.

5 CHALLENGED
Each student is challenged academically and prepared for success in college or further study and for employment and participation in a global environment.

THE WHOLE CHILD

The ASCD Whole Child approach is an effort to transition from a focus on narrowly defined academic achievement to one that promotes the long-term development and success of all children. Through this approach, ASCD supports educators, families, community members, and policymakers as they move from a vision about educating the whole child to sustainable, collaborative actions.

Teaching with Clarity relates to the **supported** and **challenged** tenets.

For more about the ASCD Whole Child approach, visit **www.ascd.org/wholechild.**